TERROR BY CONSENT

PETER LANG
New York • Washington, D.C./Baltimore • Bern
Frankfurt am Main • Berlin • Brussels • Vienna • Oxford

Lori J. Underwood

TERROR BY CONSENT

The Modern State and the Breach of the Social Contract

PETER LANG
New York • Washington, D.C./Baltimore • Bern
Frankfurt am Main • Berlin • Brussels • Vienna • Oxford

Library of Congress Cataloging-in-Publication Data
Underwood, Lori J.
Terror by consent: the modern state
and the breach of the social contract / Lori J. Underwood.
p. cm.
Includes bibliographical references and index.
1. Legitimacy of governments. 2. State, The. 3. Social contract.
4. Terrorism—Political aspects. I. Title.
JC497.U63   303.6'25—dc22   2007005749
ISBN 978-0-8204-8627-7

Bibliographic information published by **Die Deutsche Bibliothek**.
Die Deutsche Bibliothek lists this publication in the "Deutsche
Nationalbibliografie"; detailed bibliographic data is available
on the Internet at http://dnb.ddb.de/.

Cover design by Joshua Hanson

The paper in this book meets the guidelines for permanence and durability
of the Committee on Production Guidelines for Book Longevity
of the Council of Library Resources.

© 2007 Peter Lang Publishing, Inc., New York
29 Broadway, 18th floor, New York, NY 10006
www.peterlang.com

All rights reserved.
Reprint or reproduction, even partially, in all forms such as microfilm,
xerography, microfiche, microcard, and offset strictly prohibited.

Printed in the United States of America

For Hannah and Andrew and their grace that instills a yearning for a peaceful tomorrow.

Contents

Chapter One: Terrorism and Governance by Consent 1

Chapter Two: The State of Nature 17

Chapter Three: Forming a Civil Society 42

Chapter Four: Civil Foundations for Terrorism 70

Chapter Five: Rogue States 84

Chapter Six: Illegitimate Responses to Terrorism 99

Chapter Seven: A Return to Legitimacy 112

Bibliography 135

Index 139

Chapter One

Terrorism and Governance by Consent

> There is nothing more dangerous than to build a society, with a large segment of people in that society, who feel that they have no stake in it; who feel that they have nothing to lose. People who have a stake in their society, protect that society, but when they don't have it, they unconsciously want to destroy it.
> —Martin Luther King Jr.

The goal of this work is to examine the phenomenon of terrorism as a product of violated or illegitimate social contracts. In the course of this examination several theoretical explanations of social contracts will be presented and explored. Each explanation will be evaluated based on the soundness of the underlying suppositions and the feasibility of the theory given the ideological and technological realities of the modern world. It is my hope that this process will lead the reader to a better understanding of the nature of civil governance and the limits of its legitimacy.

Terrorism can be better understood, and therefore better combated, by coming to an understanding of the fundamental assumptions that ground civil society and how those assumptions can be illegitimately inverted and corrupted. Before it is possible to explore connections between violations of the social contract and terrorism, it is necessary to clearly define the important terms involved. In its simplest form, a social contract is an agreement by a people to be governed according to a set of conditions. Theoretical descriptions of the agreement differ greatly from philosopher to philosopher, and the differences are in no way trivial. Nevertheless, this definition captures the essence of a social contract in a fairly straightforward and uncontroversial way.

By contrast, defining terrorism, even in an elementary way, is neither straightforward nor uncontroversial. Many have argued that whether an act is an act of terrorism is purely a matter of perspective. One man's terrorist is another man's freedom fighter. This may be true, to an extent, if terrorism is fundamentally a reaction to abuses of the social contract. Even if this point is granted, however, there must be some basic characteristics that terrorists and freedom fighters share that are not common to normally functioning roles in just societies. My goal here will not be to distinguish terrorists from freedom fighters, but to look beyond perspective and ideology to find the essential elements of the actions that fall under these headings.

Walter Laqueur, a terrorism scholar, asserts that there are more than one hundred definitions of terrorism and that the "only general characteristic generally agreed upon is that terrorism involves violence and the threat of violence."[1] This core characteristic, however, is of little use in analyzing modern terrorism and its social and civic foundations. Many social institutions involve violence and the threat of violence, particularly when violence is broadly construed. The maintenance of standing armies, the practices of domestic and international policing, engaging in warfare or even parenting in much of the world fall under the category of terrorism this broadly construed.

Other writers have attempted to narrow the definition. Some define terrorism as any sustained effort to coerce by fear.[2] This does resolve some of the difficulties with characterizing terrorism as any activity that involves violence and the threat of violence by introducing the key element of intent. To qualify as terrorism, an action or program for action must be a directed effort to coerce. Such generally violent activities as an emergency amputation required to enact a rescue or knocking an individual unconscious to prevent them from harming themselves in a manic state could not be placed under the heading of terrorism with this clarification because there is no explicit or implicit attempt in them to coerce by fear. The inclusion of intent greatly improves this definition of terrorism.

However, the definition is still problematically broad because it includes not only the actions of organizations such as al-Qaeda, but also most penal systems. Penal codes are designed to make criminal activity undesirable by meting out harsh consequences. Similarly, secondary schools and universities enforce honor codes with threats of academic failure or expulsion. Because level of education is so closely tied to economic viability in modern society, such threats are often more coercive than physical violence. Both of these systems use fear of punishment to coerce people into avoiding criminal or unethical activities. Though it may be unfortunate that motivation to act in accord with social and ethical norms often requires coercion, it is not the case that all use of coercion is terroristic in nature. In this light, the definition requires further clarification.

The League of Nations Convention in 1937 defined terrorism as "all criminal acts directed against a State and intended or calculated to create a state of terror in the minds of particular persons or a group of persons or the general public." This definition has the benefit of excluding the types of cases discussed above. Imprisonment for violation of penal codes or expulsion for violating an honor code would not fall under the umbrella of terrorism. The definition is deficient, however, in that it does not encompass state-sponsored terrorism or attacks against subgroups within a state rather than a state itself. In January of 2006, members of Hamas won sweeping victories in Palestinian parliamentary elections. Hamas is a militant Islamist group widely believed to be a terrorist organization and has repeatedly refused to acknowledge the right of the State of Israel to exist. It seems spurious to suggest that if Hamas passed a law legitimating attacks on Israeli targets, actions that would have previously been considered terrorist attacks would transform into legitimate acts of war (such as the launching of rockets into Israel, etc.). Appeal to international law may ameliorate the concern with defining terrorism as criminal activity, but such appeals do not address the distinction between domestic and international attacks.

Consider the Freedom Riders of the American Civil Rights movement. In 1960, the U.S. Supreme Court ruled that segregation in interstate travel was illegal. Still, many states in the South did not alter their laws to reflect this decision. On May 4, 1961, a group calling itself the "Freedom Riders" set out from Washington D.C., to ride the interstate bus system to New Orleans. Members of the group were beaten in Rockhill, South Carolina, and on May 14 in Anniston, Alabama, they were met by a mob of more than 100 people. Local law-enforcement authorities in Anniston had informed the local Ku Klux Klan that it could attack the group without fear of legal repercussion. One of the buses was firebombed, and the passengers were attacked by the mob outside.[3]

What was the goal of these attacks? The goal clearly seems to have been to coerce Americans wishing to change the status quo into not seeking the enforcement of the Supreme Court's ruling in *Boynton v. Virginia*. Though there are vastly divergent perspectives concerning the intended targets of these actions, they seem to be specifically directed toward a group within the state rather than the state as a unified political body. Many in Alabama saw themselves as preserving rather than attacking the true American way of life. Still, most Americans now view these acts as terroristic (though many southerners at the time considered the attackers to be freedom fighters). Further clarification is needed.

The United Nations Office on Drugs and Crime offers an even more precise definition of terrorism by rightly observing that terrorism cannot be defined by its targets.[4] To say that terrorists attack only nonmilitary targets would be to exclude the Rhein-Main Air Base bombing in Frankfurt, Germany, in August 1985; the 1996 attack on the Khobar Towers military complex in Saudi Arabia; and the October 2000 attack on the USS *Cole* in Yemen. To suggest that these were not acts of terrorism is not only counterintuitive, it undermines the complexity of the phenomenon itself. The identity of who attacks or whom is attacked does not determine whether the act is terroristic. Rather, there must be something inherent to the acts themselves, be it in the motivation or means of execution, that distinguishes terrorism from its ideological counterpoint, freedom fighting.

A. P. Schmid, a researcher at the Centre for the Study of Terrorism and Political Violence at the University of St. Andrews in Scotland, provides an "academic consensus definition" of terrorism that has been adopted by the UN Office on Drugs and Crime.

> Terrorism is an anxiety-inspiring method of repeated violent action, employed by (semi-) clandestine individual, group or state actors, for idiosyncratic, criminal or political reasons, whereby—in contrast to assassination—the direct targets of violence are not the main targets. The immediate human victims of violence are generally chosen randomly (targets of opportunity) or selectively (representative or symbolic targets) from a target population, and serve as message generators. Threat- and violence-based communication processes between terrorist (organization), (imperiled) victims, and main targets are used to manipulate the main target (audience[s]), turning it into a target of terror,

a target of demands, or a target of attention, depending on whether intimidation, coercion, or propaganda is primarily sought. (Schmid, 1988).[5]

Though dense and complex, this definition does capture the essence of terrorism. It accounts for the contingencies not covered in the previously considered definitions and provides a solid framework for categorizing terrorist activities and for diagnosing some of the root causes of such activities. In particular, the definition addresses two important aspects of intent in regard to terrorist attacks. The motivation is "idiosyncratic, criminal or political," and the direct victim of the violence is not the main objective of the activity. Agreement or disagreement with the idiosyncratic or political motivation accounts for the distinction between the terrorist and the freedom fighter. Moreover, the clarification of the intended target versus the direct victims of the attack gives us the tool to distinguish terrorist acts from other types of exercises in violent coercion. For these reasons, Schmid's definition will serve as the standard definition for this work.

A Brief History of Terrorism

Having established a working definition for terrorism, it is important to briefly consider the history of the phenomenon. The term "terrorism" was coined during the French Revolution. The systematic execution of all those presumed to be enemies of the republic came to be known as the Reign of Terror. Robespierre remarked: "If virtue be the spring of a popular government in times of peace, the spring of that government during a revolution is virtue combined with terror: virtue, without which terror is destructive; terror, without which virtue is impotent. Terror is only justice prompt, severe and inflexible; it is then an emanation of virtue."[6] Robespierre's words are yet another example of the intimate connection between the concepts of terrorism and freedom fighting; they reinforce the importance of motivation in distinguishing between the two.

Though "terrorism" is a relatively modern term, the phenomenon itself is not solely modern. There are numerous instances of terror attacks in the ancient world. A significant number of documented examples of terrorism in antiquity are directed toward the only superpower of that time, Rome. That the greatest military power with the most far-reaching political influence was also the most frequent target of terrorism is not incidental. Historically and ideologically, there is an intimate connection between the exercise of power and terrorist attacks. One early documented example occurs in A.D. 68. At that time, the Roman port of Ostia was set ablaze by people described as "pirates." They obliterated a fleet of Roman warships and kidnapped two senators. Some scholars argue that it was the response of the Roman people to this attack that sowed the seed for the transition of Roman governance from democracy to dictatorship.[7]

Another group in the first century A.D., the Zealots of Judea, undertook a prolonged campaign to assassinate members of the occupying Roman forces and any Jews they considered to be supporters of the Romans.[8] This qualifies as terrorism under Schmid's definition insofar as the motivation was a perceived contradiction between religious and political ideologies under Roman rule. It is important that the reaction to that conflict was violent. Furthermore, the primary targets of these actions were not the direct victims of the acts, but rather the Roman occupying forces and their Jewish supporters at large.

In the late 13th century A.D., a splinter group from Shia Islam called the Nizari Ismalis came to be known as the Assassins. The group, based in northern Iran, would send individual assassins to eliminate prominent enemies of its cause. Those assassins would remain with the bodies of their victims at the sacrifice of their own lives. This display of courage and devotion inspired great fear and dread of the group.[9] Again, Schmid's definition fits the Assassins because their primary intention was to alter the attitudes of their ideological adversaries as a whole and the direct victims of the attacks were only a means to that end. Plus, their motivation was idiosyncratic. Their desire was to have their group, too small to wage war in standard ways, be feared and respected by any who would oppose it.

During the medieval period in the Western world, there was little if any recognizable terrorism. There were numerous military powers, but none arose as a superpower for any significant span of time. Thus there was no single overlord-type state to incite sustained acts of terrorist rebellion. Moreover, this being the time period of the Crusades and the rise of the chivalric worldview, most noteworthy instances of political or religious disagreement led to open warfare.[10] One notable, though not ultimately realized exception to this trend is the 1605 Gunpowder Plot in England. Guy Fawkes and four other conspirators plotted to blow up Parliament. Their ultimate goal was to assassinate King James I and his court so that England could be reclaimed for Catholicism.[11] This fits Schmid's definition of terrorism in two ways. First, the motivation for the attack was religious ideology. Second, the intended effect was not primarily on those who would be killed, but on the larger group that supported the Scottish (and, more important, the Protestant) regime in England. The Gunpowder Plot conspirators wanted not only to rid England of James Stewart but to make England seem undesirable for any aspiring Protestants who would replace him.

In the 19th century, the Industrial Revolution ushered in the modern era and with it a resurgence of terrorist activity. As the working classes left rural areas and surged into cities to find employment, cultural clashes and ideological differences intensified. Early on, most terrorism was domestic. Anarchists and other political ideologues used violence to pursue their goals. No longer tied stringently to political ideologies of church or feudalism, a political and religious pluralism developed, particularly in the West. That pluralism contributed to small-scale battles between groups on the fringe of societies and the societies they wished to alter.

As the sophistication and availability of weapons technology increased in the 19th and 20th centuries, there was a marked increase in international terrorism. Rising media penetration made it possible for extremists to garner great effect from destruction on a relatively small scale. Thus groups were able to target larger populations to witness and fear their acts of violence. Not incidentally, the 20th century saw the rise of two superpowers and the fall of one. The United States and the Soviet Union spread their influence through military force across the globe. The Soviet Union fell in the last years of the century, but the escalation of weapons technologies fueled by decades of competition between these two nations reshaped the global political landscape and gave rise to the variety of terrorism with which most of us are most familiar today.

Trends in Modern Terrorism

Now, in the early 21st century, the influence of terrorism on global consciousness is pervasive. Stories abound concerning missing weapons-grade nuclear materials and the proliferation of biological arsenals. Since the attacks of September 11, 2001, the United States and Europe assess the level of terrorist threat almost daily. Reports of terrorist plots and of successful assaults are part of daily media exposure. On March 11, 2004, the Basque separatist group ETA bombed three Madrid train stations, killing at least 173 people. Dozens were killed and hundreds injured when a series of bombs exploded at Underground stations and on buses in London on July 7, 2005.

In the 2006 report to Congress, *Trends in Terrorism*, Raphael Perl identified several changes in the nature of terrorist activity since the 9/11 attacks and the subsequent invasions of Afghanistan and Iraq. Global terrorism in 2006 is marked by an increase in the number of "micro-actors", or small decentralized militant cells. There is also a higher level of sophistication in the planning and execution of attacks as well as a greater collaboration between terrorists and organized crime syndicates. And while there has been a decrease in state-sponsored terrorism, there has been an increase in suicide bombings connected to the U.S. military operations in the Middle East.[12]

The continuing evolution of terrorism brings with it both an escalating anxiety and a spark of hopefulness. Though modern technology and decentralization expand the potential for great harm, there seems to be an increasing level of commitment among the nations of the world to at least withhold support for those who would resort to abhorrent tactics to settle ideological disputes. However, this growing unity of opposition must be viewed with great caution. Just as there is a clear distinction between the absence of hostilities and true peace, there is a tremendous difference between withholding support for terrorist groups and attacking the militant approach to conflict resolution that underlies it.

The banality and savagery of modern-day terrorism have led the United States and some of her allies to embark on a self-proclaimed "global war on terror." Proponents of the struggle often argue that the conflict is a holy war, a *jihad*. Both religious devotees and anti-religious intellectuals have made the case for a strong causal relationship between religion and terrorism. In his book, *The God Delusion*, Richard Dawkins argues that religious zealotry is the only reasonable explanation for numerous acts of terrorism and that this is but one example of how religion is inherently harmful to societies.[13] As has been noted, the keys to identifying terrorism are intent and motivation. While it is true that terrorism has often been motivated by religious conviction, it would be a mistake to isolate religion as a primary cause for terrorism.

Terrorism and Religion

The belief that terrorism is primarily caused by religious extremism is not well supported. While high–profile organizations such as Hamas, al-Qaeda, and the Jemaah Islamiya have clear ties to religious radicalism, there are abundant examples of groups without directly motivating religious affiliations. The diversity of ideological incentives among these groups underscores the need for both a more comprehensive definition such as Schmid's and for remedies to terrorism that focus on root societal causes rather than particular motivating ideologies. The diversity of ideological motivation is best illustrated by example.

The Liberation Tigers of Tamil Eelam, better known as the Tamil Tigers, are a separatist group in Sri Lanka originally formed in 1976. They subscribe to Marxist ideology as interpreted by Lenin and are committed to the establishment of a separate state for ethnic Tamils. In the course of the conflict between the Sri Lankan government and the Tigers, it is estimated that at least 69,000 people have been killed; 4000 of those since the ceasefire agreement in 2002.

Another Marxist-Leninist separatist group identified as a terrorist organization by the United States is the Kurdistan Workers' Party (PKK). Primarily comprised of Turkish Kurds, the faction began a violent campaign in 1984 for the establishment of an independent Kurdish homeland in Turkey. As many as 30,000 people have died in the conflict, many in attacks on tourist sites and hotels. They are also known for kidnapping foreign tourists.[14]

The Basque Fatherland and Liberty, known as ETA, was formed in 1959 with the goal of establishing an independent Marxist state in the Spanish Basque provinces. Bombings executed by ETA have claimed the lives of at least 800 and thousands more have been injured.[15] Though the Madrid train bombings in March 2004 were attributed to ETA as an act of Islamic extremism, the primary goal of the group remains political.

Despite the fact that terrorist groups have demonstrably divergent motivations for their activities, there is a common thread. Whether seeking religiously or ethnically unified societies, all of these organizations are actively withdrawing themselves from the boundaries of the social contracts uniting their existent societies. All flagrantly withhold their consent to be governed in a manner contrary to their cherished ideologies.

Clearly, terrorism is one of the primary concerns in the contemporary Western world. This primacy requires a reexamination of the essential aspects of living in a civil society. If the nations of the world are to cure an illness of this magnitude, they must first understand the nature of the body politic. The most fundamental characteristics of any political body arise from the agreement that holds that political body together. Such agreements may be implicit and simply handed down from generation to generation or they may be made explicit by means of a constitution or comparable document. Whatever the form, the agreement lays out the conditions under which a people will come together to form a society. The agreement is, in essence, a consent to be governed.

The Social Contract: Governance Only by Consent

> Men being . . . by Nature, all free, equal and independent, no one can be put out of this Estate and subjected to the Political Power of another, without his own Consent.
> — Locke, *Second Treatise of Government,* VIII: 95

By what authority is a people governed? What gives one, or many, the right to govern others? Wherein does ultimate sovereignty lie, and how is that sovereignty transferred? What are the limits of legitimate governance? These are just some of the questions that have been answered by social contract theorists including Thomas Hobbes, John Locke, Jean-Jacques Rousseau, Immanuel Kant, and John Rawls. Though they disagree about the appropriate manner and justification for governance, all of these theorists agree that authority to govern is always granted by the governed. In other words, no individual or collective of individuals is governed except by its own consent.

Initially, the claim that people are not governed except by their own consent seems counterintuitive. History is rife with examples of political oppression and tyranny. Surely that is compelling evidence that peoples can be ruled without their consent. To suggest otherwise seems to fly in the face of common sense. I believe the counterintuitiveness of the consent-to-be-governed claim is ascribable to two central misconceptions.

The first is that rule by military force implies rule without consent. This is grounded in the erroneous assumption that those who participate in the military are soldiers first and citizens second. Thus, their duties to follow orders given by superiors supersede their implicit duties as members of a body politic. Though this may happen in the course of human events, the inference to the conclusion does not hold upon close scrutiny. It is vital to avoid the pitfall known as the naturalistic fallacy. It is groundless to claim that what ought to be can be derived solely from what is the case in practice. To suggest that following the orders of a military superior takes precedence over meeting civic duties ignores the relationship of logical priority that exists between the two. For a soldier to gain a station as the military arm of the state, there must first be a state. That soldier must consent to a part of the *civitas* not temporally before (since there is implicit agreement to identify with one's *civitas*), but methodologically before serving as a military agent. Since military duties would be nonexistent in the absence of civic duties, it is reasonable to infer that civic duties take precedence over military duties. Consequently, the military cannot externally force a people to be governed, because each member of a military (except perhaps foreign mercenaries, but these that are virtually nonexistent in the modern era) is first and foremost a citizen of the society being governed.

The second misconception is that consent implies the absence of coercion. That one has a compelling reason to consent does not imply that consent is absent. Consider as an example the soldier who is captured and tortured by the enemy. He knows that his suffering will end if he reveals sensitive security information about his homeland. He is certainly experiencing drastic coercion, but the presence of that coercion does not prevent the soldier from withholding his consent to reveal sensitive information. Will most individuals give in to torture and be coerced into cooperation? Empirical evidence strongly suggests that the answer is yes. However, there are individuals who withhold their consent in the direst of circumstances. That being the case, there is necessarily a distinction between the presence of coercion and the absence of consent. An individual or group of individuals may refuse to consent to be governed, even though the consequence of such refusal may be death.

Having clarified the feasibility of the claim that governance happens only by consent, it is important to turn to the expression of that consent: the social contract.

On the Nature of the Social Contract

The means by which a people express their consent to be governed is the social contract. A social contract (also known as a compact) is essentially an explicit or implicit agreement between those who would be governed and those who would govern. Whether all parties involved, or merely the governed, are bound by the contract varies depending on the expression of that particular contract. There are many theoretical assumptions that affect how a given contract will be expressed. Such assumptions include the nature of man, the demands that will be made on the sovereign, and the conditions that would exist in the absence of a social contract. These will be addressed in greater depth as different theories of the social contract are explored in the following chapters.

Each social contract determines the limits of legitimate governmental authority for that society. The contract will establish whether the primary responsibilities of the governors will be external security, internal security, social control, settlement of disputes, clarification of property rights, or some combination of these. In legal terms, the social contract can be a grant of powers or a limitation of powers, depending on the particularities of each contract. A society that makes its social contract a limitation of the sovereign's power sets down the parameters of governing power negatively: "The governors may do what ever they like so long as they do not do x, y, or z." A society that makes its contract a grant of powers gives the governors a specific set of duties and authorities, and the governors may only act in ways and to the extent explicitly sanctioned in the original agreement. Totalitarian governments tend to function under a limitation-of-powers social contract, whereas republican governments tend to function under grant-of-powers agreements.

Limitations of Powers and Grants of Powers

Two historical examples may further clarify the distinction between agreements that grant powers and those that limit powers. The first is Louis XIV of France, the Sun King. Like most of the monarchs who believed themselves to rule by divine right, Louis XIV would have rejected the very notion of a social contract. Divine-right rulers believed themselves to have been chosen to rule by God, and the will of the people was ancillary to that fact if not completely irrelevant. That being acknowledged, the government of Louis XIV functioned like an extreme version of a limitation-of-powers social contract. Louis could do as he pleased so long as he did not make living conditions in his society such that anarchy or revolution seemed superior to consenting to be governed by one's king (divinely chosen or otherwise). Another way of saying this is that Louis' only limitation was that he was not allowed to create a life for his subjects worse than their life would be in the state of nature. It is also important to note that Louis' refusal to acknowledge that he was functioning according to a social contract does not invalidate the assumption that the contract was present. Some social contract theorists do not require that governors enter into the contract at all. It is the governed who agree among themselves to give up a subset of their natural rights and to cede those rights to a governor. This is a Hobbesian notion of the social contract that will be more fully explicated in later chapters.

The second historical example is Richard M. Nixon, 37th president of the United States, and it will illustrate the grant-of-powers type of social contract. Nixon was elected president in 1968 and was reelected in 1972. Following the exposure of his attempts to cover up the Watergate break-in, Nixon was charged with three crimes: obstruction of justice, abuse of power, and contempt of Congress. On August 9, 1974, Nixon resigned the presidency to avoid the expected loss of an impeachment vote in the House of

Representatives and an ensuing trial in the Senate.
Consider the following excerpt from the House motion to impeach:

> In all of this, Richard M. Nixon has acted in a manner contrary to his trust as President and subversive of constitutional government, to the great prejudice of the cause of law and justice and to the manifest injury of the people of the United States. (Approved 28-10 by the House Judiciary Committee on July 29, 1974)

The motion to impeach makes it clear that U.S. presidents are bound by a contract that grants rather than limits their powers. That the United States delegates authority to governors as a grant of powers is made explicit in the Tenth Amendment: "The powers not delegated to the United States by the Constitution, nor prohibited by it to the states, are reserved to the states respectively, or to the people." As president, Nixon was granted certain powers in addition to those generally held by members of the body politic. He was granted specific powers as governor, as enforcer of the social agreement between his fellow citizens. Attempts to exercise powers not specifically given were deemed "subversive of constitutional government" and therefore an illegitimate exercise of power. It was not that Nixon violated a negative requirement of his rule (something to the effect of "Do not use your office to undermine justice"). Rather, the injury was that Nixon exercised powers beyond those specifically granted to U.S. presidents.

The distinction between a limit-of-powers social contract and a grant-of-powers social contract may seem trivial at first because a wide range of contracts could be negotiated under both models. Indeed, some limit-of-powers social contracts can be quite expansive in their limitations, just as grant-of-powers social contracts can be very generous in the degree and nature of power granted to governors.

Governmental Legitimacy

The first question that must be answered when examining governmental legitimacy is whether the contractors are delegating or ceding power. In a grant-of-powers social contract, the governor or governors must themselves be party to the founding contract. These kinds of contracts are more common in rule-of-law societies, but they may also be found in rule-of-man societies. Examples of the former include most republics and democracies; examples of the latter include constitutional monarchies. In all of these examples, the governor agrees to not exceed the powers granted to him and is bound by the terms of the contract, even if he is not bound by the same set of obligations as the other members of the society. The governor implicitly agrees to return his delegated powers to the body politic that delegated them if ever he tries to exercise powers beyond those granted in the contract. Governmental actions are legitimate only to the extent that those actions fall within the parameters of granted contractual powers.

In the United States, a primary function of the U.S. Supreme Court is to adjudicate questions of governmental legitimacy. The Court is made up of justices rather than judges because its role is not to apply a body of law to specific cases but to determine whether actions of executives, legislators, and other members of the judiciary are just. In other words, the Court asks, Do those actions fall within the limits of legal legitimacy as expressed in the Constitution, the document that expresses the essential social contract of the people of the United States? In many societies, however, the judiciary does not play a central role in refining, and at times redefining, the limits of governmental legitimacy. Societies that have built their societies around a civil-law model (as opposed to a common-law model like that of the United States) tend to rely less on the judiciary and more on legal scholars when debates about governmental legitimacy arise. Both of these strategies for refinement and redefinition, however, are intended to be primarily interpretive. These strategies and others like them are directed toward maintaining at least the core qualities of the underlying agreement that holds a given society together.

Many Visions of the Contract

As mentioned previously, there is not a single, unified vision of what a social contract is. Philosophers have debated the matter for centuries without reaching consensus. In the chapters that follow, some of the major visions of the social contract will be explained and evaluated. The final chapters will look at those concepts of the social contract as they relate to the historical and contemporary practices of human governance. Based on this analysis, I will offer a set of fundamental contractual components that I think are essential to any just and sustainable society. Grounding my approach in the contractarian tradition, I will propose strategies for ameliorating terrorism by fostering governmental legitimacy.

Notes

[1] Walter Laqueur, *The New Terrorism: Fanaticism and the Arms of Mass Destruction* (New York: Oxford University Press, 1999), p. 6.
[2] Ibid.
[3] King Encyclopedia at (www.stanford.edu/group/King/about_king/encyclopedia/freedom_rides.htm).
[4] United Nations Office on Drugs and Crime at (www.unodc.org/unodc/terrorism_definitions.html).
[5] Ibid.
[6] Maximilien Robespierre, *Report upon the Principles of Political Morality Which Are to Form the Basis of the Administration of the Interior Concerns of the Republic* (Philadelphia, printed and sold at no. 112, Market-Street, 1794. OCLC: 17637510).
[7] Robert Harris, "Pirates of the Mediterranean," *New York Times*, Sept. 30, 2006.
[8] Terrorism Research (http://www.terrorism-research.com/history/early.php).
[9] Ibid.
[10] Ibid.
[11] Antonia Fraser, *Faith and Treason: The Story of the Gunpowder Plot* (New York, Anchor Press, 1997).
[12] CRS: Congressional Research Service, *Trends in Terrorism: 2006*, July 21, 2006 at (http://fpc.state.gov/documents/organization/69479.pdf).
[13] Richard Dawkins, *The God Delusion* (Boston: Houghton Mifflin Company, 2006)
[14] Country Reports on Terrorism, Released by the Office of the Coordinator for Counterterrorism April 30, 2007 (http://www.state.gov/s/ct/rls/crt/2006).
[15] Ibid.

Chapter Two

The State of Nature

Social contract theory has often been criticized as being predicated on false assumptions, namely that there ever was a state of nature and that people in that state made an explicit agreement to exit it and enter civil society. These objections take two general tracks, the first religious and the second empirical.

Notable among those critics who object to the underlying assumptions of social contract theory based on biblical interpretation is Sir Robert Filmer. In *Patriarcha*, Filmer argues that a state of absolute liberty for humans never existed. Such an idea, he says, is unnatural and dangerous because it disrupts the true natural order of things and leads to such transgressions as usurpation and revolt. God's creation of Adam was concurrently the creation of absolute monarchy. God created Adam as ruler over all other creations, and his lordship was to be passed down from first son to first son. Thus, humans never lived in a state of liberty. From the beginning, there was a ruler, and all others were his subjects. Since humans were born into this governmental structure as ordained by God, there was never total liberty or the authority to give or withhold consent to be governed.[1] John Locke takes Filmer to task for this line of reasoning, and his objections to Filmer helped lay the groundwork for Locke's own social contract theory.

Other critics have taken a more scientific approach. They argue that there is simply no evidence that humans ever lived outside of social structures. Anthropological evidence shows social organization in even the earliest societies. Though such organization was in most cases tribal in nature, there was nevertheless a clear leadership structure and enforced social roles. Moreover, humans are essentially social animals, and even the most fundamental social elements, families, operate according to enforced social rules. If there was no state of nature qua perfect liberty, then there cannot have been an agreement to leave that state and enter civil society. In the absence of any supporting evidence, this line of reasoning goes, it is unreasonable to base a justification for governance on such assumptions.

Anticipating such criticisms, Hobbes contended that even if there was no state of nature in all parts of the world, it was certainly present in some. In fact, Hobbes argued that something very close to the state of nature was present among the natives of America during the time he was writing Leviathan in the mid-17th century.[2] It seems that Hobbes's answer is largely predicated upon his ignorance of the organizational structures of Native American tribal societies. Hence, even if his rebuttal was compelling to his contemporaries, it is unlikely to convince modern critics advancing this objection.

These objections would provide good reason to question the viability of social contract theories if indeed those theories required the existence of an actual state of nature and an explicit compact to exit that state. Fortunately, social contract theories need not rely on an actual state of nature as a foundation. It need not be the case that rational agents chose to exit the state of nature to be governed in a specific way. It need only be the case that such agents would make those choices if given the opportunity. In other words, a metaphorical state of nature is a sufficient ground for these theories. Since we are talking of normative and not descriptive conditions for governance, what would be chosen has as much authority as what actually was chosen.

The reasoning behind the metaphorical state of nature construct lies in the logical priority that exists between person and state. Because the existence of persons is a necessary precondition for the formation of a state via a social contract, it makes sense to consider what might compel prepolitical individuals to band together as a political state. There can be no agreement to form a body politic if there are no individuals who can enter into an agreement. Imagining a set of prepolitical individuals as a body of informed deliberators allows us to discern what the relations between individuals and state should be.

Moreover, the metaphorical construct allows reconsideration of the terms of the contract in light of new knowledge and social conditions. What a group of rational agents would choose as the limits of governance in a time of great poverty, ignorance and desperation may well not apply when those conditions change. Thus it is acceptable to concede the possibility that there never was a state of nature without ceding the viability of social contract theory as a suitable normative framework for determining the terms of legitimate governance. In what follows, I will provide an explanation of different frameworks from major figures in the history of social contract theory.

Hobbes

Hobbes's Political Context

One of the earliest contractarians was Thomas Hobbes, a prominent figure in the early Enlightenment. To understand the Hobbesian vision of the state of nature, it is first necessary to understand certain assumptions Hobbes makes concerning metaphysics. Traditional Aristotelian thought held that the universe was made up of objects at rest that had to be set in motion. Since everything in motion had to be set in motion to bring it out of its initial state of rest, there must exist a prime mover that initiated the change from rest to motion. Galileo rejected this notion, instead positing that the natural state of all things was motion and that there had to be forces applied to objects to bring them from motion to rest. The universe is essentially mechanistic, Galileo thought, and all individuals within the universe are simply matter in motion. Hobbes was fascinated with this new approach to metaphysics, and after meeting Galileo in 1636 Hobbes began applying this conception of natural law to human affairs.

Hobbes's political writings were published during an exceptionally chaotic period of British politics that had taken root a century earlier. In 1534, Henry VIII signed the Act of Supremacy, making himself head of the Church of England and officially severing all ties with Rome. Twelve years later, Henry's son, Edward VI, became king, and in his short reign he endorsed Protestantism and passed laws that further unsettled the social infrastructure of an England that had been Catholic for many generations. When Mary I ascended the throne in 1553, she reinstated the Catholic bishops and instituted a period of Protestant persecution in England. In 1558, when Elizabeth I assumed the monarchy, she repealed all of her half-sister's Catholic legislation, and under her guidance in 1563 Parliament passed the Thirty-nine Articles, which fully established the Anglican Church. Elizabeth was succeeded in 1603 by James I (James VI of Scotland), a passionate Protestant and firm believer in the divine right of kings. His son,

Charles I, came to power in 1625 and continued to perpetuate the idea of divine right. He had a number of conflicts with Parliament and was eventually arrested and executed in 1649. Civil war ensued between those loyal to Charles II and those loyal to Oliver Cromwell, and in 1653, Cromwell, a Puritan, assumed rule of England as Lord Protector. In 1659, Cromwell's son and successor, Richard, was forced to resign, and in 1660 Charles II was restored to the throne. The conflict of these competing forces along with Hobbes's time as tutor for the banished Charles II shaped and reshaped his vision of the social contract.

In 1640, Hobbes published *Elements*, which gave his view of the nature of humankind and of sovereignty. He fled for Paris that same year, fearing that his text showed favor for a monarchy that would likely not prevail in the raging civil war. It was during this time that he served as tutor for the future Charles II. His next work was *De Homine and De Cive*, Man and Citizen, in 1642 which more fully explained the status and nature of civil government. The work seemed far more applicable to the seemingly stable monarchy of France than to the chaotic flux of English politics. So in 1651, Hobbes returned to England and published *Leviathan*, considered to be his magnum opus. By 1666, Hobbes's views on politics, geometry, and religion had him embroiled in conflict with members of the Royal Society. The king interceded on his behalf but would not allow Hobbes to publish any more philosophical works in England.

The Nature of Man

The brutal discord and variability of sovereign authority in his time is reflected both in Hobbes's view of human nature and his structure for civil society. He begins *Leviathan's* theory of governance with a theory of nature that echoes Galileo's mechanistic account. According to Hobbes, all human thought originates in the senses, and imagination is nothing more than decaying sense; memory is another word for imagination. What we would call lower-order reason, Hobbes describes as an elementary form of understanding. Since it arises from imagination, this simple form of understanding can be found in both human beings and beasts because both are built to store senses.[3]

Common experience teaches us that animals remember past experiences. An animal that has been mistreated will behave erratically or nervously in circumstances similar to those under which the abuse took place. In a more scientific arena, the ability of nonhuman animals to store senses in what Hobbes calls "imagination" is evidenced by the famous Pavlovian experiments with dogs. Pavlov was able to cause dogs to salivate at the sound of a ringing bell. He accomplished this by training the subjects to associate the sound of a bell with the appearance of food. Eventually, the dogs would salivate at the sound of the bell even when no food was presented. It was not the direct smell of food that caused salivation, but the recall of previous senses that occurred when the bell was rung. An interesting secondary component of the experiments that lends further support for Hobbes's assertion that nonhuman animals can store senses is the fact that if the bell was rung and no food presented for a number of consecutive times, the dogs would "unlearn" the salivating behavior.

In addition to this basic understanding, humans have the ability to form trains of thought called "mental discourse." Mental discourse can be unguided, or it can be regulated by a desired end. Prudence and the ability to reason from cause to effect and effect to cause are nothing more than manifestations of imagination, which is itself entirely grounded in sense. It is only in the development and diligent use of language that humans demonstrate what is categorized as higher reason. In this regard, people and beasts are different not in kind but in degree. All objects in the universe are only matter in motion, but God teaches Adam speech, thus allowing humans a distinct status.

> There is no other act of man's mind, that I can remember, naturally planted in him, so as to need no other thing to the exercise of it but to be born a man, and live with the use of his five senses. Those other faculties, of which I shall speak by and by, and which seem proper to man only, are acquired and increased by study and industry, and of most men learned by instruction and discipline, and proceed all from the invention of words and speech. For besides sense, and thoughts, and the train of thoughts, the mind of man has no other motion; though by the help of speech, and method, the same faculties may be improved to such a height as to distinguish men from all other living creatures.[4]

As to the nature of the motion that moves man and beast, there are two kinds: vital and voluntary. Vital motion is the involuntary movement of blood, air, and so on that is required to sustain life. Voluntary motion is the result of desire. It is from desire that Hobbes forms his conceptions of good and evil. Whatever is desired is good, and whatever is hated is bad. Good and evil mean nothing more. There is no universal good or evil that can be used as a standard for rational agents to settle disputes. "There being nothing simply and absolutely so; nor any common Rule of Good and Evill *[sic]*, to be taken from the nature of the objects themselves."5

Life in the State of Nature

Because all humans are the same sort of creature and because all of their qualities are derived from senses common to all, all humans in the state of nature are naturally equal. Even if one is particularly strong or particularly intelligent, when all things are considered all humans have equal power and equal liberty to claim any object of their desire.

Imagine a collective of people constrained by no rules of conduct and no independent standards of good and evil. In such conditions, even if one individual has physical strength that greatly exceeds that of those around him, another will have wit, beauty, or some other trait that will unite the others into a coalition against him. And because standards are reducible to individual desires or aversions, there is no objective standard to which an appeal can be made for definitive resolution. Thus, this state of complete liberty and complete equality leads inevitably to conflict.6

In sum, because all have equal power to attain what they desire and because there are not infinite objects to desire, humans in the state of nature must be in constant competition. In the context of this constant competition, no one is ever secure in his possessions or in his ability to actualize desires for future goods. This leads to unremitting and pervasive fear and anxiety. Without an overarching power to control humans, life in the state of nature degrades into a state of constant warfare; a war of all against all, "and the life of man, solitary, poore, nasty, brutish and short."7

But if indeed humans have the ability to reason, why can't this state of constant warfare be stopped by appealing to a shared sense of justice? Many theorists argue that reason alone can lead an agent to an understanding of the objective status of right and wrong and thereby to an understanding of justice. If agents in the state of nature were able to have such an appeal, they would need no external power to enforce justice upon them. But for Hobbes and his adherents, this appeal to objectivity is suspect because reason is necessarily subjective.

Recall that reason is nothing more that a repetitive exercise of imagination, which is itself nothing more than degrading stored sense data. If all that people have experienced is a state of constant warfare, they would not have a foundation that would enable them to make distinctions between their current state of existence and an alternative state of existence that has any positive characteristics. What is more, Hobbes defines justice as necessarily connected to civil law. In the absence of law, there can be no justice. "The notions of Right and Wrong, Justice and Injustice have there no place. Where there is no Common Power, there is no Law: where no Law, no Injustice."[8]

If it cannot be positive notions of right or justice that lead people out of the state of nature, it must be something in their own set of sense experiences. All have experienced the urge to flee danger, and all have been faced with the necessity of taking steps to preserve their own lives. From these experiences in the vile state of nature, Hobbes builds a formula for constructing the artificial man, the body politic into which they will immerse themselves. This is the formula for the Leviathan, the civil state that will save people from their own natures.

In sum, for Hobbes all humans are machines (albeit divinely crafted machines) whose functions rely solely on the gathering and processing of sense data. Based on these data, humans develop their reason to acquire their desires and avoid those things they find undesirable. Because all humans operate in this way, all have equal power to attain their desires and equal liberty to claim them. This equality, combined with scarcity of goods, leads to constant warfare. Warfare puts people in a state of anxiety, fear, and insecurity that molds for them an existence of perpetual abject misery in which there is no time for artistry, philosophy, or anything other than an endless battle for survival.

Locke

Locke's Political Context

John Locke does not share Hobbes's dire account of the essential nature of man and his behavior outside the constraints of civil society. Some of Locke's greater optimism is likely traceable to the greater political stability in Britain in the era immediately preceding his publication of the *Two Treatises of Government*. Although struggles over religion continued, the increasing influence of Enlightenment thought helped to ameliorate the tensions and brought greater reliance on discourse than on armed conflict. These experiences seem to have helped shape Locke's vision of humankind's rational nature and the importance of a balanced power structure in a just society.

Locke was just ten years old in 1642 when the English Civil War erupted. For much of his youth, England was a commonwealth under the Cromwells. He later witnessed the conflicts that accompanied the restoration of the king and the Bill of Rights Act of 1689 making England a constitutional monarchy. Even when the English people saw fit to again remove a reigning king from power, they were able to do so without war or execution. Throughout his lifetime, Locke saw an England in flux; moving toward the progressive republic embodied in Locke's political writings.

After his restoration to the throne in 1660, Charles II dealt with a number of confrontations between his Catholic and Protestant subjects. Charles had no legitimate heirs, and when he died in 1685 he was succeeded by his younger brother James, a practicing Roman Catholic. James II's ascension to the throne brought great anxiety to a United Kingdom that had identified as Protestant for more than 100 years. There was also great fear that the religious persecutions that plagued the reigns of the Tudor monarchs would be reenacted. This fear was exacerbated when James made grants of religious toleration known as declarations of indulgence and made the Abbey Church of Holyrood into a Roman Catholic Chapel Royal. When James had a son in June of 1688, there was concern that another Catholic dynasty would occupy the throne of England. In response, William of Orange (husband of James's daughter Mary) was encouraged by prominent Protestant statesmen to invade. William and his army landed in June of that year and marched on London without challenge. William promised to protect England and Scotland and their Protestant identity, and so Parliament denounced James, who fled to France. To preserve the line of succession, William III and Mary II were made co-regents. This was known as the Glorious Revolution because it ended without the death of the deposed king.

In addition to the political climate of the time, Locke was influenced by Filmer's writings. Filmer was a stalwart royalist who was imprisoned for a time during the English Civil War. A critic of Hobbes, Filmer argued that usurpation of a monarch could never be legitimate. He died in 1653, but his manuscript *Patriarcha* was published posthumously by the Tories in 1680. Locke wrote the Two Treatises largely to refute Filmer's arguments.

The Nature of Man

Locke argues that, contrary to Filmer's account, humans are not born into a state of slavery. Though Locke was a man of faith, he opposed divorcing revelation from reason. Thus modes of revelation such as scripture must be contemplated and interpreted in the context of our existence as rational, thinking beings. He rejects Filmer's arguments not because they are religiously grounded, but because they have irrational implications. Filmer writes:

> I see not then how the children of Adam, or of any man else, can be free from subjection to their parents. And this subjection of children being the fountain of all regal authority, by the ordination of God himself; it follows that civil power not only in general is by divine institution, but even the assignment of it specifically to the eldest parents, which quite takes away that new and common distinction which refers only power universal and absolute to God, but power respective in regard of the special form of government to the choice of the people.[9]

Locke presents numerous arguments against Filmer's view, but one is of particular importance in establishing Locke's positive view of the essential nature of humans. Locke maintains that Filmer has set up a self-defeating dichotomy. If monarchical power passes from Adam through his sons, then one of two situations must exist. Either there is only one rightful king on earth to whom all owe allegiance (because each first son has himself only one first son) or inheritance of authority is not limited to first sons. If there is only one rightful heir of Adam, then all must withhold allegiance until it is determined who that is. Since this cannot practically be done, allegiance (and thus slavery to the monarch) must be withheld indefinitely. So, in practice, all men are free and not enslaved. If multiple sons of Adam may inherit, then all may inherit by the same line of reasoning. Since all men now living are sons of Adam, all inherit sovereignty and none are slaves.[10]

Consequently, Locke begins his positive account of human nature with a rejection of intrinsic servitude and an affirmation of intrinsic freedom. The natural state of humans is

> a state of perfect freedom to order their actions and dispose of their possessions, and persons as they think fit, within the bounds of the Law of Nature, without asking leave, or depending upon the will of any other man.[11]

Human beings' natural state is also a state of complete equality. All people are of the same species and, as such, have equal claim to dominion over themselves and their property. If God wills that a people be made subjects to another, he will make it known by a clear act.[12]

To this point, Locke is largely in agreement with Hobbes. Humans in the state of nature enjoy both perfect freedom and absolute equality. Unlike Hobbes, however, Locke sees limits on human action as an intrinsic part of the state of nature. Locke argues that the law of nature is authored by God and necessarily conforms to reason. Because the law of nature conforms to reason, it can be discovered by using reason. By discovering God's moral law, reason sets limits on human behavior in the state of nature. This approach works only because Locke defines human rationality in a far richer sense than Hobbes does.

Locke writes that reason is "the discovery of the certainty or probability of such propositions or truths, which the mind arrives at by deduction made from such ideas, as it has got by the use of its natural faculties; viz, by the use of sensation or reflection."[13] As to the nature of knowledge, Locke classifies it as reason's perception of agreement or disagreement between ideas.[14]

Whereas Hobbes sees reason as a composite of sense experiences via the storage of those experiences in the imagination, Locke sees reason as a human faculty. Part of what it is to be rational is to be human. It is not the case that we learn to be rational through experience. Instead, we are able to learn from experience only by using reason. Human reason provides boundaries for actions in the state of nature. Thus, even though the state of nature is a state of perfect liberty and perfect equality,

> it is not a state of licence: though man in that state have an uncontroulable *[sic]* liberty to dispose of his person or possessions, yet he has not liberty to destroy himself, or so much as any creature in his possession, but where some nobler use than its bare preservation calls for it.[15]

The state of nature is ruled by the law of nature, and that law is reason itself. Reason tells us that unless we are in extraordinary circumstances such as self-defense, there is no justification to ever harm another in any way. We may not harm the health or threaten the life of another person, damage or take the property of another person, or constrain another person's liberty. Reason demands this because it reveals that we are all creations of God who are sent here to do God's will with equal authority. And because all have equal status as creations and equal authority of purpose, there is no reason to think that one person's will should submit to another's. Thus the liberty that exists in the state of nature as it is constrained by reason is the liberty to do as we please to the extent that in doing so we do not harm the liberty, health, or property of anyone else.[16]

It is Locke's establishment of reason as a constraint on the exercise of liberty that distinguishes his view of essential nature of man from Hobbes's. Humans are able to limit the scope of their actions without appeal to an overarching external force. Consequently, Locke has a significantly different depiction of life in the state of nature.

Life in the State of Nature

Locke provides an image of man in his natural state as a rational and therefore moral agent who pursues his own ends without unfairly compromising the ends of other agents within his sphere of influence. This creates a state of nature that is essentially stable and peaceful. It is a far cry from the Hobbesian war of all against all. Such a peaceful state of nature is made possible by the authority of reason as established by a rational God.

Because of human rationality, there are distinctions between right and wrong and thus between justice and injustice in the Lockean state of nature. As Locke acknowledges, people do not always behave in accordance with their rational natures. The law of nature, which sets the division between justice and injustice, would be meaningless if there were no mechanism by which it is enforced. So by virtue of the equality of all people, all people have the right and the responsibility to punish those who violate the law of nature, but only to the extent that future violations are deterred.

The only circumstance in which one person may justly harm another is to punish violations of the law of nature. This justified harm must be undertaken rationally and dispassionately, and it must be proportional to the initial offense and be designed to deter future offenses.[17] This right to inflict justified harm belongs to all people. In addition, one who has been the victim of an act that violates the law of nature has the right to do harm to the person or property of the offender to the extent that is necessary for reparation. In the case of murder, there can be no reparation. Moreover, a murderer has shown himself to be a threat to all people in that he does not listen to the call of reason on the most fundamental terms. Murderers, therefore, are to be executed and the execution is both just and necessary.[18]

Because humans have free will and are thereby able to choose to violate the law of nature, it is possible to have a state of war. There are those that will choose to pursue the destruction of another, either by seeking the other's death or the subjugation of his liberty and property. When this happens, the aggressor and the intended prey are in a state of war with one another along with allies that join either side.[19]

Even after war has been declared, though, strict boundaries exist between what is just and unjust. The aggressor has made a choice to abandon the law of nature and behave as a beast and not a rational human. These actions are unjust. The object of the aggression is justified in seeking the destruction of the assailant. Because the assailant has abandoned the call of reason, this human being can be put down for the protection of others as a wild beast would be.

Unlike Hobbes, Locke draws a stark contrast between the state of nature and a state of war. In the state of nature, people live rational lives that are therefore peaceful and harmonious. A state of war ensues only when rationality is abandoned. Once a state of war is declared, harm tends to lead to further harm until there seems to be no disinterested authority to resolve the matter. In such conditions, where there is no recognized unbiased judge of what is lawful, the only appeal the combatants have is to the justice of heaven. The desire to have an earthly authority to whom disputants can appeal gives people cause to sacrifice some of their natural liberty to enter into civil society.[20]

Another motivation for entry into civil society is the desire to protect and preserve property. Locke derives the unalienable right to property as a logical implication of human existence. When a person is born, that individual has a right to preserve the life that he or she has been granted. To that end, God gives dominion over the earth and all of its nonhuman inhabitants to all people in common. God grants reason to people so they will know how to use what has been given. Embedded in this is the notion of stewardship. Our fellow human beings, both now and in future generations, share equally in the inheritance of the earth. Because of this equal inheritance, no one is justified in abusing the earth or the goods it provides. We are to take what we can use responsibly and leave enough for others to meet their needs. Reason also reveals that the earth can only meet our needs with effort on our part.

To claim as one's individual property a part of what has been given to all, one must mix one's labor with that part in a way that removes it from its natural state.

> Whatsoever then he removes out of the state that nature hath provided, and left it in, he hath mixed his labour with, and joined to it something that is his own, and thereby makes it his property. It being by him removed from the common state nature hath placed it in, it hath by this labour something annexed to it, that excludes the common right of other men: for this labour being the unquestionable property of the labourer, no man but he can have a right to what that is once joined to, at least where there is enough, and as good, left in common for others.[21]

This means that when Andrew hunts a deer, kills it, removes and cooks its flesh, and tans its hide, that meat and hide become Andrew's property and no one else's (though Andrew may disperse his property to others as he sees fit). Similarly, when Hannah gathers fallen acorns or picks wild berries and prepares and eats them, those acorns and berries become her property.

But just as with liberty, there are limits to the amount of property that any one individual may claim. Since the earth is given to all as common property, no one can take more than his share. That means that enough must be left behind for all, and that all must have access to resources of equal quality. This rewards industry without condoning greed. The difference between the two can be derived by the employment of reason.

From the need to store labor (since the goods of the earth are often perishable) comes the use of money. Money, however, has value only through the mutual consent of those agreeing to exchange it. Moreover, this ability to store labor tends to lead to the gathering of more private property than is needed. The need to establish a defined value for money and the need for a reliable and disinterested process to settle property disputes gives those in the state of nature another motivation to enter civil society.[22]

To summarize, life in the state of nature according to Locke is a state of equality and liberty. That liberty is constrained by a rational understanding of the equality of all. Reason provides a standard of justice that can mitigate disputes. It is only resolution of disputes in times of war and the need to regulate and adjudicate property ownership that leads people to enter into civil society.

Rousseau

Rousseau's Political Context

The Enlightenment ideals that took root in European thought in the time of Hobbes and Locke blossomed in the 18th century. Science and philosophy became part of the public discourse, and new models of governance and economics were debated and embraced by progressives. The France that Jean-Jacques Rousseau entered as a young man was markedly different from the France of the previous century. In 1715, when Rousseau was a small child in Geneva, King Louis XIV died after a 72-year reign, and the crown of France passed to the 4-year-old Louis XV. For the next 9 years,

The State of Nature 31

France was governed under the regency of Philippe, duke of Orleans. Philippe restored the right of remonstrance to the Parlement, setting the standard for a parting of ways with the ideal of divine right monarchy. When Louis XV assumed governance in 1723, France found herself ruled by a child of the Enlightenment who appreciated science and valued progress.

Though Louis was well educated and cultured, he was neither as aggressive nor as decisive as his great-grandfather. By the mid-1740s, a series of libel campaigns left the public with an image of an inept and financially irresponsible king. The image of the monarchy had transformed from one of absolute authority to one of minimal competence. It was in this period of transformation that Rousseau entered the French intellectual stage. Enlightenment ideals and disillusionment with monarchical governance helped to shape his political ideology.

The Nature of Man

Among all major contractarians, Rousseau provides the most succinct summation of his view of man's essential nature: "Man is born free; and everywhere he is in chains."[23] The freedom to which Rousseau refers is the freedom of the state of nature. In his natural state, a person who had reached the age of discretion is the only one suitable to decide how he ought to behave. To remove oneself from the state of nature is to renounce liberty, and for a man to renounce liberty is to renounce his essential nature.[24]

In response to those who argue that not all men are equal because some are born to rule and some to be ruled, Rousseau asserts that there has been confusion between cause and effect. People became enslaved and knew no better than to accept slavery as their appropriate condition. "Force made the first slaves, and their cowardice perpetuated the condition."[25]

Like Hobbes and Locke before him, Rousseau believed that man in the state of nature is completely free and enjoys full equality with all other people. There are no external forces that naturally constrain human prerogative. In contrast with his priors, however, Rousseau did not think that the decision to enter civil society justified abandoning these natural qualities.

Life in the State of Nature

In Rousseau's thought, the state of nature is a state of freedom and harmony. Rousseau makes a distinction between social relationships and civic relationships. Families are the earliest societies, and among social structures they are the only one that is natural. Authority and obedience in these natural societies are transient; as soon as the need for protection and supervision dissolves, so do the bonds of obedience. If parents and children decide to remain together after the need to give and receive care is gone, they do so voluntarily—there is no debt of obedience. The social uniting of individuals capable of independence is convention, not nature. Thus we must conclude that the natural state of man is one of independence and freedom. Obedience and dependence are natural only for those of insufficient development to sustain themselves.[26]

Civil society is a perversion of the natural society found in families. In families, a father's reward for caring for his children is his love for them. In civil society, a ruler's reward for caring for his subjects is the pleasure he takes in commanding them. Moreover, any condition of servitude is unnatural, and to enter into civil society is to become a subject—a servant.[27]

For Rousseau, no law of nature would ever require us to abandon the state of nature for civil society. Since entry into the state of nature is not necessitated by any rational choice, it must be nothing more than convention. It is possible to imagine conditions in which the obstacles to sustaining oneself in the state of nature become burdensome. It is to relieve those burdens that free people agree to live together in a civil society. They cannot, however, choose to live together in a society with a set of rules that abandons any natural freedoms.[28] To give up liberty is to become a slave, and slavery is antithetical to personhood.

The apparent contradiction between entering civil society and rejecting slavery leads Rousseau to his notion of the general will. Humans can enter civil society without becoming slaves only if they maintain sovereignty in the transition. As will be more fully explained in the next chapter, the general will allows humans to exit the state of nature without enslavement.

Kant

Kant's Political Context

Immanuel Kant was born in Königsberg, Prussia, in 1724. For most of Kant's adult life, Frederick II of Prussia, who was known as Frederick the Great, ruled Prussia. Frederick, who was celebrated for his great military prowess, was also an accomplished intellectual who entered into philosophical correspondence with a number of French philosophers, including Voltaire. He embraced the principles of the Enlightenment view and eschewed draconian approaches to governance. Frederick wrote a treatise criticizing Machiavelli titled *Antimachiavell*, which was published by Voltaire in 1740.[29]

It is likely that Kant's experiences with Frederick's rule combined with his lifelong residence in Prussia shaped his views of civil society and the state of nature. Kant saw civilization as the proper state for humans, and his political and moral writings suggest that he believed men in a civilized society could make admirable progress toward "the ultimate kingdom of ends."

The Nature of Man

Kant has a complex account of human nature. His Critical System provides explications of human knowledge, moral reasoning, and faculties of judgment. To give a complete account of Kant's views on human nature would be prohibitively lengthy, so for present purposes I will give a brief summary and request pardon for the important subtleties that will be left out.

Man, for Kant, is a finite rational being with a capacity for theoretical understanding that is limited to a specific set of categories. Beyond these categories, man may speculate but not attain theoretical knowledge. Moral knowledge, on the other hand, can be accessed without the same mediation. The access to and utilization of moral knowledge is the cornerstone of human freedom. Humans have the freedom to choose to obey the moral law and act contrary to our desires.

Knowledge of the moral law is, according to Kant, the fourth and final stage of human reason. The first stage of reason is the simple move beyond instinct. In this capacity, reason led people to experiment in their habits of acquiring foodstuffs. Rather than being solely driven by instinct, man varied his diet except where doing so contradicted instinct. This employment of reason is the source of the varied nature of human desires. The second stage of rationality was an exertion over the immediacy of desire. In this second stage, man refuses his desires, not because of the call of the moral law, but for the purpose of moving from animalistic sexual instincts to prolonged attitudes of love. In this stage, man develops a sense of decency; he concludes that one ought to treat others with good manners so as to enhance social interaction. The third stage of reason is the anticipation of the future. It is in this stage that humans begin forming life plans rather that living merely moment to moment. The final stage of reason is the stage at which man realizes he is an end in himself because he is able to resist his desires for the sake of doing what is good. He comes to understand the moral law and consequently his intrinsic value as a possessor of a good will.[30]

Only the good will is inherently valuable because it embodies the freedom to choose moral action over the determinations of our natural desires.[31] Moral actions are constrained by three laws or, rather, three formulations of the one moral law. Because of our finitude, we must comprehend the moral law as an imperative—as an "ought" rather than an "is." These rules are the three formulations of the Categorical Imperative. They are as follows. No one may perform an action unless it is rational to will that everyone perform that action. It is impermissible to ever treat any person merely as a means to an end. Finally, we should do our best to act in a way people would act in an ideal society, in an ultimate kingdom of ends.[32]

Kant argues that all three formulations of the Categorical Imperative are expression of the same, unified moral law, but that our finite rationalities require us to analyze them separately. The kingdom of ends formulation is perhaps the most mysterious, but also the most relevant in political terms. Our respect for others and desire to act on rationally universalizable maxims instill in us a duty to work toward a society that treats members morally.

Because the freedom to choose moral action and the pull of our desires is the source of our moral value, we have an implied right to exercise that freedom without unwarranted coercion. That is to say, we have the right to act as moral agents. In Kantian terms, our inner freedom to choose moral actions implies a right to outer freedom from coercion that would prevent us from doing so. It is the lone original right and from it all other rights are derived. Though inalienable, the right to exercise freedom without coercion from an external will has inherent limits in virtue of its source.

Even though all people (absent disease or defect) are capable of reason, not all people are, in practice, rational. Young children, women, and some men cannot, or do not, embrace their own rationality. Since it is reason that gives humans their intrinsic value, an individual who does not take up her rational nature commits the ultimate transgression against her own nature. Children, of course, are off the hook as they are not yet able to utilize their capacity for reason. In "What Is Enlightenment?" Kant writes:

> Enlightenment is man's emergence from his self-imposed immaturity. Immaturity is the inability to use one's understanding without guidance from another. This immaturity is self-imposed when its cause lies not in lack of understanding, but in lack of resolve and courage to use it without guidance from another.[33]

Whether Kant includes women in his account of personhood is an open question, but I believe that he does, given other remarks in this essay. I believe Kant sees the immature rationality of women as a product of social conditions and not as an intrinsic property.

> The guardians who have so benevolently taken over the supervision of men have carefully seen to it that the far greatest part of them (including the entire fair sex) regard taking the step to maturity as very dangerous, not to mention difficult.[34]

The precise composition of the moral community aside, for Kant, all who are capable of moral agency as described above have the same right to exercise that agency; this right is not to be compromised except to the degree necessary to maintain compatibility with the exercise of the same right by all other agents. This means that I may exercise my right to determine the course of my own actions only so long as I do so in a way that is compatible with the same exercise by all rational beings. Constraints on actions are internal, from one's own access to reason, and not external. It is the right to external freedom that lays the groundwork for Kant's theory of governmental legitimacy.

From the preceding, it follows that Kant, like Rousseau and Locke, sees reason as the defining attribute of human beings. Far more than his predecessors, however, Kant emphasizes that weakness of will (akrasia) can hinder the actualization of human reason. Each of us has a duty to fully realize our abilities as rational agents.[35] This duty plays a key role in the exit from the state of nature.

Life in the State of Nature

Even though Kant believed that humans are rational prior to any experience (and indeed, rationality is a condition for the possibility of experience) and that moral knowledge follows directly from reason, his view of the state of nature is comparable to Hobbes's. Kant agrees with Hobbes that in the state of nature, no ends can be accomplished (other than that of exiting the state of nature) with any means other than war.

> In the absence of this critique reason is, as it were, in the state of nature, and can establish and secure its assertions and claims only through war... As Hobbes maintains, the state of nature is a state of injustice and violence, and we have no option save to abandon it and submit ourselves to the constraint of law, which limits our freedom solely in order that it may be consistent with the freedom of others and with the common good of all.[36]

Kant's agreement with Hobbes is, I think, closely tied to his position that there are other intrinsic properties of human beings that do not conform to reason. Humans are rational, but they are also drawn, by their nature, toward warfare. Because Kantian man is rational in a stronger sense than is Hobbesian man, the state of nature is not necessarily a state of constant war (injustice), but it is a state where justice cannot exist because war is the only means to conflict resolution.[37]

> This facility in making war, together with the inclination to do so on the part of rulers—an inclination which seems inborn in human nature—is thus a great hindrance to perpetual peace.[38]

Human passions lead them toward war, whereas their reason leads them toward peace and justice. It is this internal conflict that leads humans to abandon the state of nature and its corresponding state of perpetual warfare. Each individual realizes that it is his rationality that makes him alone capable of good. He then recognizes that good demands justice, and finally that justice is only possible in civil society.[39] It is not only a selfish desire for self-preservation, but also a sense of moral duty that leads man away from the state of nature and into civil society.

Rawls

Rawls's Political Context

John Rawls was born in the United States in 1921. As an American, he was immersed in a culture that espoused the often competing values of capitalism and a democracy founded on the ideal that "all men are created equal." The implicit tension can be seen as an underlying motivation for Rawls's political theory.

Rawls witnessed both the desolation of the Great Depression and the prosperity of the postwar era of the late 1940s and 1950s. His experiences with such vastly different circumstances of wealth and scarcity almost certainly motivated his search for a stable and philosophically grounded theory of justice. Because prosperity or poverty seem arbitrarily predicated on accidents of birth (when was one born, to whom, and with what natural abilities), there must be some account of justice that balances the scales for all people, because all have equal moral value.

The Original Position

Unlike his contractarian predecessors, John Rawls did not set out to determine the conditions under which a people came to be in a given civil society. Instead, he seeks to set out the conditions under which any agreement to be governed would be just and therefore legitimate. This is similar to Rousseau's goal in The Social Contract, but whereas Rousseau bases his account of the limits of legitimate governance on human beings' natural state, Rawls sets aside empirical questions about human nature and instead focuses on a hypothetical state, which he calls the Original Position.

The Original Position is a thought experiment that can be used to establish the central tenets of a just social contract. Since the goal is justice for all and not the advancement of personal interests, individuals in the state of nature are to place themselves behind a "veil of ignorance." Behind this veil, the participants do not know whether they will be "advantaged or disadvantaged by natural fortune or social circumstances."[40] They are also ignorant of any specifics about their role in society, so they cannot "tailor principle to the circumstances of one's own case."[41] Finally, all are unaware of their particular ambitions and notions of what is good and valuable. Note that this is not a general concept of good, but rather the specific idea of what is good for the individual. It is an instrumental kind of good that is dependent upon the circumstances and goals of a particular rational life plan.

The veil of ignorance is designed to prevent participants from skewing the principles of justice toward their own benefit. Suppose I were an intelligent, petite brunette woman from the middle class who particularly loves chocolate-covered strawberries. I might create a society in which, for example, tall blonde men are required to do all domestic chores (with a required competence in the cultivation of strawberries and the manufacture of fine chocolate), and in which brunette females with above-average IQs are guaranteed first choice at educational and vocational opportunities.

Without the veil of ignorance, there is a problematic temptation to create standards of justice that reward individuals with properties and circumstances similar to one's own. In doing so, there is inevitably a disadvantage for anyone with other attributes and tastes. Clearly, no society that delegated advantages and disadvantages so arbitrarily would be just in any meaningful way. Therefore, the veil of ignorance is necessary.

Again, this is a thought experiment, so those participating must check themselves to be sure the veil is being maintained. If it is, a disinterested third party would be able to judge that any rational person ignorant of the particulars of their own natural and social circumstances would assent to the principles chosen. Ignorance of circumstances, however, is not the only requirement for the Original Position.

All parties in the Original Position must be equal. That is to say, all have equal authority to propose potential principles, de-

The State of Nature 39

bate the merits of proffered principles, and to contribute to a final decision on whether a given principle will be adopted. This equality is necessary because it represents the inherent moral equality of all people.[42]

It is important to stress that the equality enjoyed by all people is not a literal or even practical equality as suggested by Hobbes or Rousseau. Even Locke's account of equality comes from a "natural" source, namely inheritance from Adam. Rawls recognizes that people are not, in fact, equal. Some people are intelligent, charismatic, and beautiful, whereas others have low to modest intelligence and socially repellent behaviors and appearance. It is because people are not naturally equal that society has a duty to make them morally equal.

Parties in the Original Position must also be adequately rational. All must have "the requisite ability to understand and act upon whatever principles are adopted."[43] Otherwise, the principles would not be the product of a sound rational debate, and they may not be practically achievable. In either case, a proper account of justice for real societies will not have been reached.

In sum, Rawls relies on a hypothetical Original Position and not a theoretical account of what man is like in his natural state to ground his conception of justice. Agents making decisions from the Original Position are ignorant of their own circumstances, goals, and natural and social attributes. This ignorance, combined with adequate rationality and equality, leads to the deduction of a sufficiently vetted set of principles to establish a framework for a just society.

Conclusion

In the preceding we have seen disparate accounts of what humans might be like in their natural state. Some argue that humans are essentially animalists who seek advantage after advantage in a way that perpetuates a constant state of war. They would argue that the only way to escape the brutality of the human condition is to have human nature forcibly repressed by an external power. Others argue that humans can, by virtue of their rationality, live well in the state of nature but meet obstacles that make civil society appealing. Still others see the natural human state as both impossible to establish and irrelevant to the task of setting parameters for a just and sustainable society. The next chapter will trace the development of civic identity and obligation from the foundations set forth in accounts of the state of nature.

Notes

[1] Sir Robert Filmer, *Patriarcha and Other Writings* (*Cambridge Texts in the History of Political Thought*), ed. Johann P. Sommerville (Cambridge: Cambridge University Press, 2006).

[2] Thomas Hobbes, *Leviathan*, 3rd ed. (Cambridge: Cambridge University Press, 2000), part I, chap. 13. This is an excellent revised student version of the text. The argument concerning native Americans in the state of nature is on page 89.

[3] Ibid., part I, chaps. 1–2.

[4] Ibid., part I, chap. 3. p. 23.

[5] Ibid., part I, chap. 6. p. 39.

[6] Ibid., part I, chap. 13.

[7] Ibid. p. 89.

[8] Ibid. p. 90.

[9] Filmer, *Patriarcha,* bk. I, sec. 4.

[10] John Locke, *Two Treatises of Government* (*Cambridge Texts in the History of Political Thought*), ed. Peter Laslett (Cambridge: Cambridge University Press, 1988), *First Treatise,* chap. 10, sec. 105.

[11] Ibid., p. 269.

[12] Ibid.

[13] John Locke, *An Essay Concerning Humans Understanding,* in *Clarendon Edition of the Works of John Locke,* ed. Peter Nidditch (Oxford: Oxford University Press, 1975), IV.xviii.1 (p. 689).

[14] Ibid., IV.i.2.

[15] Locke, *Two Treatises of Government* (*Cambridge Texts in the History of Political Thought*), ed. Peter Laslett (Cambridge: Cambridge University Press, 1988), *Second Treatise*, chap. 2, sec. 6 (pp. 270–271).

[16] Ibid.

[17] Ibid., chap. 2, secs. 7 and 8.

[18] Ibid., sec. 11.

[19] Ibid., chap. 3, sec. 16.

[20] Ibid., secs. 19–21.

[21] Ibid., chap. 5, sec. 27 (p. 288).

[22] Ibid., chap. 5.

[23] Jean-Jacques Rousseau, *The Social Contract,* in *The Basic Political Writings,* trans. Donald. A. Cress (Indianapolis, Ind.: Hackett, 1987), bk. I, sec. 1.

[24] Ibid., sec. 2.

[25] Ibid.

[26] Ibid.

[27] Ibid.

[28] Ibid., sec. 6.

29 *Encyclopedia Encarta* at (http://encarta.msn.com/encyclopedia_761567792/-Frederick_II_(of_Prussia).html).
30 Immanuel Kant, *Conjectures on the Beginning of Human History*. An excellent translation is in *Kant: Political Writings* (*Cambridge Texts in the History of Political Thought*), ed. Hans Reiss (Cambridge: Cambridge University Press, 1991), pp. 221–228.
31 See Immanuel Kant, *Fundamental Principles of a Metaphysic of Morals*, first section: "Transition from the Common Rational Knowledge of Morality to the Philosophical." A version edited by Irwin Foman and Herbert W. Schneider was published by Kessinger Publishing Company in 2005.
32 For a full explication of innate right and freedom, see "The Metaphysical Elements of the Theory of Right," in Kant's *The Metaphysics of Morals*.
33 Immanuel Kant, "An Answer to the Question: What Is Enlightenment?" in *Kant, Foundations of Ethics*, trans. Leo Rauch, (Millis, Mass.: Agora Publications, Inc., 1995), p. 1.
34 Ibid.
35 Whether fully realizing his own reason leads man out of the state of nature or whether reason can be fully realized only once man has entered civil society is an interesting question for Kant scholars. Cynthia Schossberger provides an in-depth analysis of this issue and of the related issue of the permissibility of coercion in, "Raising a Question—Coercion and Tolerance, in Kant's Politics" in *ethic@,- Florianópolis*, v. 5, n. 2, pp. 165–171 December 2006. Available at (http://www.cfh.ufsc.br/ethic@/et52art3.pdf).
36 Immanuel Kant, *The Critique of Pure Reason*, trans. Norman Kemp Smith (New York: St. Martin's Press, 1965), A 751–725/B 779–780 (pp. 601–602).
37 Immanuel Kant, *The Metaphysics of Morals*, "The Theory of Right, Part II: Public Right," Section 1: "Political Right," par. 44, in *Kant: Political Writings* (*Cambridge Texts in the History of Political Thought*), ed. Hans Reiss, trans. H. B. Nisbet (Cambridge: Cambridge University Press, 1970, 1991), p. 137
38 Immanuel Kant. "Perpetual Peace: A Philosophical Sketch," in *Kant: Political Writings* (*Cambridge Texts in the History of Political Thought*), ed. Hans Reiss (Cambridge: Cambridge University Press, 1970, 1991), sec. 5, p. 196.
39 Justice presumes the enforcement of laws that cannot exist in the state of nature. Ibid., sec. 6.
40 John Rawls, *A Theory of Justice*, rev. ed. (Cambridge, Mass.: Belknap, 1999), p. 16.
41 Ibid.
42 Ibid.
43 Ibid.

Chapter Three
Forming a Civil Society

The primary assumptions of social contract theory are that people are governed by their own consent and that the terms of that consent are dictated by the essential qualities of human beings. Social contract theorists agree that, in some capacity or another, humans are rational. Rationality makes us capable of understanding our own nature and thereby our own inherent worth. Upon coming to this understanding, we are able to negotiate reasonable terms by which we will be governed by a force external (in some manner or another) to our own will. As with all negotiations, it makes no sense to negotiate oneself into a less advantageous position. For that reason, a legitimate social contract cannot compel people to live in conditions that are worse than those that would exist without the contract. Hence, there are clear connections between a philosopher's account of man's natural state and the parameters of the legitimate social contract.

Hobbes

In the previous chapter, it was established that Hobbes has an extremely dim view of man's essential nature and therefore of human behavior outside the constraints of civil society. Because of this position, Hobbes's version of the social contract gives the broadest license to the governor. The key to understanding the Hobbesian social contract lies in the distinction, discussed previously, between grants of powers and limitations of powers.

Among the social contract theorists covered in this work, Hobbes is alone in combining two social contract properties: the essential transfer of rights is a permanent transfer of powers to a sovereign who does not enter into the compact, and the resulting contract is to be seen as a limitation of powers only. Hobbes is in accord with other contractarians in maintaining that life in civil society can never devolve below the conditions in the state of nature. His state of nature is so bleak, however, that setting the bar there allows the sovereign tremendous leeway; he is prevented only from taking the life of one of his subjects without allowing the subject a chance to preserve it. Hobbes explains his view of legitimate governance in terms of rights of nature and laws of nature. Rights can be determined by examining man's nature, and laws can be understood in terms of a negative version of the Golden Rule. "Do not that to another, which thou wouldst not have done to thy selfe [sic]."[1]

Right of Nature and Laws of Nature

Before explaining Hobbes's vision of the right and laws of nature, it is important to distinguish what he intends by the terms from their more common meanings. Generally speaking, rights and responsibilities are related but distinct. The scope of our moral rights by and large corresponds to our ability to take responsibility for them, but to have a right does not necessarily oblige one to act to protect it.

For example, my right to be told the truth does not bring with it a duty to verify the veracity of all statements made to me. To undertake this duty would be cumbersome to say the least and would likely diminish my overall quality of life. Because Hobbes does not subscribe to moral realism, he does not contrast moral and political rights. Instead, he distinguishes between natural and political rights. It is important to note that this sense of natural law is amoral. It is not an appeal to a higher moral law, but rather an appeal to our own base nature.

For Hobbes, natural rights (as opposed to political ones) have corresponding duties. Humans have one inalienable right: the right to preserve their own lives. With that right comes the right to judge how to best execute it.[2] There is no impediment (external force) that would prohibit one from exercising this right. In other words, no other person has a right that limits my right to pursue my own preservation. If I decide the best way to preserve my life is to take yours, nothing (other than your ability to prevent me) restrains me from doing so. This is the case because to exercise our right to preserve our own lives, we need only our internal capacities for reason and judgment.

In the state of nature, reason and judgment are initially somewhat shortsighted. The lack of restraint on individual life plans leads to a war of all against all. In the short term, the most expedient way to meet one's own needs is at the expense of another in close proximity. However, our ability to recall and reflect on sense data eventually leads to greater prudence. Reason and judgment, when they are exercised upon the knowledge that we have a right to protect our own lives, ultimately lead us to the knowledge of two primary obligations. These are the first and second laws of nature.[3]

Because in the state of nature, no one is protected from the actions of another, we are in a state of perpetual warfare that will inevitably take our lives. So, reason dictates that we are obliged to seek peace. If war brings lives to an end, peace must preserve lives. The obligation to seek peace is the first law of nature.[4]

Reason then takes us one step further. If we are obliged to seek peace, and if unlimited liberty inevitably leads to war, then limiting that liberty is the only means to peace. Still, there is no advantage to giving up one's own rights and liberties unless all of the others in the company do the same.[5] Else the result is not an end to war, but merely surrender to one of the combatants. Such decisions to surrender may result in a temporary armistice, but the inequality in a state of equality for all will eventually lead to a renewal of hostilities.

Consequently the only means to peace is for all to give up an equal amount of liberty. This agreement to mutually give up liberties is the social compact. That we must enter into a social compact in which we retain no rights that we would not have everyone retain is the second law of nature.

There are two ways to give up rights. Rights can be abandoned, or they can be transferred. It is in this description that Hobbes makes clear that his contract is to be construed as a limitation of powers and not a grant of powers. Rights are ceded, not delegated and thus all authority over those rights lies in the hands of the individual (or group) that claims or receives them. The claimant is within his authority and is legitimately enforcing the social contract as long as he does not attempt to exercise rights that have not been surrendered. This brings us to the question of which rights a people are obliged to surrender according to the second law of nature.

Any contract that does not safeguard a meaningful right to preserve one's own life is by definition void. It is in fact the only cause other than the absence of force to compel parties to keep their promises in the state of nature that can make a contract void.

"For though a man may covenant thus, unless I do so, or so, kill me; he cannot covenant thus, unless I do so, or so, I will not resist you when you come to kill me."[6] It is self-defense that leads us into the social contract in its capacity as inalienable right, and no one would ever choose forfeiting his life if he has the alternative of trying to preserve it.

The right to preserve one's own life can only reasonably be exercised by entering into a cooperative agreement with everyone else. Since all other rights can, and are, exploited when retained by the people, the only right that the people maintain when entering into the social contract is the right to preserve their own lives in a meaningful way. The right to life implies inalienable liberties for all people including "the security of a man's person, in his life, and in the means of so preserving life, as to not be weary of it."[7]

It is important to note that Hobbes construes these rights narrowly. To live well (so as to not weary of life) does not mean to live a life of extensive liberty. To live well means to not be prohibited from meeting all basic needs. Our general intuition is that the freedom to live well implies some dominion over our own options and life plans; it is freedom to pursue what we will. Hobbes argues that these kinds of intuitions are founded upon a fundamental misunderstanding of the nature of liberty. Since humans, like all other things on earth, are simply matter in motion, to suggest that liberty implies the right to will as one pleases is misguided. Like everything else, our only force is motion, thus the only constraint on us is the constriction of our motion. In other words, liberty is a freedom from external restraint, not a freedom to will some action without coercion or determining cause.

Once the terms of the contract are set, a very important question arises: Why should any contractor trust the others in his company to keep their promise to transfer an equal portion of their rights? The promise is being made in a state of nature in which justice and injustice do not exist. If, in the state of nature, others have a right to take my possessions or even my life, then surely they have the right to lie when making a promise. It is for this reason that Hobbes declares that the sovereign, the individual who takes possession of the transferred or abandoned rights of the compacters, is not a party to the contract. The sovereign does not make any sort of binding agreement with the people. He promises nothing and transfers no rights. He simply takes the rights of the compacters and uses those rights to enforce the terms of the contract upon them.

Though he continues to exist in the state of nature, the sovereign makes possible the establishment of civil justice for those whose contract he enforces. The sovereign is the power that compels signatories (though agreement may be explicit or implicit) to the original agreement to abide by its terms. Force is necessary to establish the contract because humans cannot be trusted to live up to their end of the bargain of their own volition. If the sovereign were bound by the contract, he could not be trusted to abide by its terms. As an external force claiming the transferred rights by making no promises, however, he can be relied upon to enforce the contract because by it he gains a great deal of power and loses nothing. It is in his interest to be the executive force for the contract, and only this force prevents the contract from becoming void. Concerning contracts made in the state of nature, Hobbes writes:

> If a covenant be made wherein neither of the parties perform presently, but trust one another . . . it is void: but if there be a common power set over them both, with right and force sufficient to compel performance, it is not void.[8]

Since the right of nature and the first and second laws of nature require all in the state of nature to abandon all rights save the right to life, they may not subsequently call for liberties that extend beyond that right in any way. Just as one who has sold a piece of land cannot dictate the purposes for which that land will be used, so are the rights ceded in the social contract. Because those who abandoned or transferred their rights did so voluntarily and for their own preservation, it would be an injustice to try to reclaim them or dictate how they will be used.[9] To deny this is to violate the terms of a voluntary contract. That no one violate the terms of a contract that has been validly entered into is the third law of nature, and it is derived from the first and second. The third law establishes justice.

Justice, once established, must be made meaningful. This exposition is found in the remaining laws of nature. The fourth law of nature emphasizes that when one benefits from the goodwill of another, he should take no action that makes the other regret his goodwill. The fifth law of nature deals with camaraderie. All members of a body politic should make reasonable accommodations to others in their society. Correlatively, the sixth law dictates that we forgive the trespasses of others whenever it is reasonable to do so.

The seventh law deals with harms that cannot reasonably be forgiven without repercussion. When punishments must be meted out, they should be fair and proportional. The goal should be to make conditions better in the future, not to exercise anger for the transgression that is now past.[10] Hobbes sees civil society as the means for peace, and peace cannot be perpetuated if men retain the right to take personal vengeance on one another for wrongs. This would instigate war and rebellion. The right to punish has been given to the sovereign, and the sovereign seeks to keep order so that he may use the rights he has claimed from the people to his own benefit. Therefore, punishments are an exercise of the power of the sovereign, through the people, for the sole purpose of limiting future unrest.

For similar reasons, the eighth law of nature dictates that no one may commit contumely.[11] That is to say, no one may openly declare hatred or contempt for one of his fellow subjects. Such open animosity leads to civic unrest and is thus to the disadvantage of the sovereign. Because expression of hatred is not an integral part of sustaining one's life (and is in many cases contrary to that end), it is not a right retained by the people. For the same reasons, the people may not express pride (the ninth law) or arrogance (the tenth law).[12]

The eleventh, twelfth, thirteenth, and fourteenth laws enforce the equity maintained when exiting the state of nature. All people are naturally equal, and all give up the same rights when exiting the state of nature. Thus, equality is preserved and must be acted upon. Judges must treat all parties equally. Any goods that cannot be divided are to be used as common property. Property that can be divided, but not equally, is to be distributed by lot. The lot can be arbitrary or natural. Arbitrary lots are determined by the agreement of competitors, and natural lots are distributed by primogeniture. When other methods of division fail, the right to dispense with property is to be given to the individual that first claims it.[13] All of these laws apply, of course, only to property needed to sustain life or any additional property beyond this threshold that is given to the people by their sovereign.

The final five laws of nature pertain to matters of peacekeeping. No one may hinder or endanger a person charged with mediating peace. All parties in a conflict must submit to having that conflict settled by arbitration. The right to settle your own conflicts is abandoned when exiting the state of nature. No one can be his own judge or be judge in a case in which he has an interest. Otherwise, all parties will not be treated fairly. Finally, matters of fact must be settled by additional arguments or witnesses not party to the conflict because the judge must give equal credence to the claims of the contesting individuals.[14]

The Commonwealth

Once the laws of nature that ground the social contract are established, it is possible to consider the range of legitimate commonwealths. Hobbes sees the commonwealth as an artificial person founded upon the consent of those within. And the commonwealth, with the sovereign as its head, "may use the strength and means of them all, as he shall think expedient, for their peace and common defence."[15] Because the people have ceded all rights save the right to preserve their own lives, they have no say in the form of government instituted by the sovereign who has claimed the forfeited rights. He may govern in any way he sees fit, and he may transfer any or all of the rights he has claimed in any way he deems appropriate.

Hobbes allows that there are three kinds of commonwealths: monarchy, aristocracy, and democracy. The power to rule is the same in all cases; the only difference is whether the power is invested in one, in some, or in all. Although all of these can be legitimate forms of government, Hobbes sees monarchy as inherently superior. Because humans are disposed to infighting and seeking their own benefit to the detriment of others, the monarchy is the most efficient form of government. Only in a monarchy is there a unified will that is not subject to disagreement with itself.[16] The rights of the sovereign are comprehensive, indivisible, and eternal.

The sovereign makes any laws he pleases, makes war or peace with other nations as he sees fit, and determines the conditions under which his people live (so long as they are given the liberty to preserve and defend their own lives). There is no action the sovereign can take that will cause him to forfeit the rights he has claimed. Those rights may be transferred to another by choice or claimed by another in conquest. In either case, the people are bound by the original contract to the new sovereign and have no right to protest. The people cannot accuse the sovereign of injustice, because justice applies only to those bound by the contract, and the sovereign is not party to the contract. Unless he contracts with others, he remains in the state of nature and thus by definition cannot act unjustly. Because he cannot act unjustly, he cannot merit any punishment from his subjects.[17]

In sum, men need to submit themselves to the absolute power of the commonwealth to control their own base natures and avoid perpetual war. Given human nature, it is irrational to preserve any right for all other than the right to life. Though many forms of commonwealth may exist, the monarchy is the best because it most efficiently preserves the commonwealth by preserving the peace among the people. Sovereign authority is all but absolute. A sovereign may exercise all rights that were abandoned by the people when the commonwealth was formed, and he may exercise them in any way that pleases him. His power may not be guided by the people or reclaimed by the people. The contract is eternal, and power may be passed from sovereign to sovereign by conquest or succession without any interference from the people. Hobbes puts the strictest limits on the right to revolution. There is no right to revolt, but the people may make a new contract if they ever again find themselves in the state of nature (abandoned by all sovereigns).

Locke

For John Locke, the right to revolution is much broader because far more rights are preserved by the people upon entry into civil society. Any infringement of those preserved rights not only justifies but demands action on the part of the people. Locke argues that political power brings with it the duty to exercise that power within prescribed limits. When a government fails to remain within those limits, power automatically reverts to the people.

Remember, for Locke civil society is needed to prevent war, to establish a stable value for money, and to settle property disputes. People in the state of nature can resolve other matters by appealing to the principle of justice. The fundamental distinction between the formation of Locke's commonwealth and Hobbes's is in the nature of the handover of powers.

Initial Transfer of Power

Whereas for Hobbes, powers are permanently transferred to the sovereign, for Locke the people authorize the commonwealth to serve certain functions. This is a grant-of-powers social contract. Consent to the social contract can be explicit or tacit. One tacitly agrees to the terms of a social contract by accepting a share of the authority to govern that results from the formation of that society. Simply living in a society and obeying its laws does not imply consent to the contract.[18] One must claim the right to delegate and exercise legislative, judicial, or executive power in the society to consent to its contract. Exercises of power may be as immense as rulership, or as simple as casting a vote to choose agents to exercise government authority.

These agents may use only the powers that the people authorize them to use and only under the terms of the authorization. Any other exercise of power by the civil state is strictly prohibited and illegitimate. To make the limitations and terms meaningful, all governors are party to the social contract. They agree to the terms under which power is delegated, and they tacitly agree to return that power to its authors should the terms of the contract be violated. It is the responsibility of the citizens of a commonwealth to curtail the unwarranted use of power.

> For hereby he authorizes the Society, or which all is one, the Legislative thereof to make Laws for him as the publick *[sic]* good of the Society shall require; to the Execution of which his own assistance (as to his own Decrees) is due.[19]

Legitimate Exercise of Delegated Power

All legitimate governments, according to Locke, function according to the will of the majority.[20] Just as a physical body will stay at rest or move in one direction or another depending upon the strongest force acting upon it, so civil societies must move as the preponderance of force demands. This is so because all civil societies are formed by the consent of those who are to be governed, and the body politic is essentially the sum of their wills. The force that directs a civil society is the will of the majority. To enter into the social contract is not to abandon one's will entirely, but rather to submit one's will to the will of the majority.

Legitimate societies have the preservation of property as their principal aim. This means the establishment of clear laws, the appointment of impartial judges, and the selection of an agent or agency to enforce just laws and make them meaningful.[21] To accomplish this aim, people entering into a civil society give up specific kinds of rights. They give up the right to pursue any life plan they please and the right to punish offenses against them. But since no one reasonably enters into a worse condition than he left, he only gives up the rights to determine life plans and punishments in such as way as advances the public good.[22]

As to what form a government may legitimately take, Locke claims that any form other than absolute monarchy is acceptable. Because the act of entering civil society is an authorization of authority and not a permanent transfer, absolute monarchy is not a legitimate form of government.[23] Absolute monarchs function in the state of nature and use whatever power they are able to access to suit their own needs. (Only those in the state of nature have absolute liberty.) Civil society is created to serve the needs of the people and is therefore inconsistent with the goals and functions of an absolute monarch.

Hereditary monarchy, elected monarchy, oligarchy and democracy are all valid. However, authority ultimately resides in the hands of the people and once the terms of the delegation of authority have been fulfilled the power reverts to the people. They may then delegate the power to another and change forms of government if they see fit.[24] This aspect of Locke's view likely embodies England's mood at the time. The people of England saw religious unrest as contrary to the common good. Since James II's ascension to the throne was seen as a harbinger of renewed religious unrest, his rule exceeded the authority granted by the people. As such, the people of England were within not only their rights but their obligations to the commonwealth to remove James II and place William III and Mary II on the throne.

Legislative, Federative, and Executive Roles and Limitations

Because what motivates the entry into civil society is the need for stable and enforceable laws, the supreme power in a legitimate civil society is the power to legislate. That power, though supreme, cannot be exercised arbitrarily. Human beings naturally have complete power to seek their own good, and they enter into society to seek their collective good. No one can allocate authority they do not possess; thus, a legislative authority cannot be granted beyond that which seeks to provide for the common good.[25]

Because the primary motivation for entering into society was the protection of property, no legislative agent or agency can take property from someone without that person's consent. A ruler or parliament can, and must, regulate property by law, but neither can take all or part of the property of citizens of the commonwealth.[26] If governors can take property, they have a motivation for making laws that are in their own interest rather than in the people's interest.

For the same reason, power to make laws cannot be transferred to another body by the individual or group in which the people initially invested the authority.[27] Otherwise, the power to legislate could be seen as a commodity to be bartered for the benefit of the legislator. This would infuse purposes into government that are not narrowly focused on the good of the people. For reasons previously outlined, this is antithetical to the essential nature of a just society.

Laws are only meaningful when they can be enforced and protected from external assault. Hence, in addition to a legislator, society requires executive and federative authorities. Executive power is delegated for the purpose of implementing the laws passed by the legislative body. Federative power is the power to make war, peace, treaties, and so on to protect the body politic from all foreign threats.[28] Even though the powers are distinct, Locke did not think they had to be placed in the hands of distinct individuals. The duties do not compete in a manner that would foster a detrimental conflict of interests.

There is, however, a detrimental conflict of interests when legislative and executive powers are assigned to the same body.[29] Legislative power is supreme, and it is the role of the executive to implement the dictates of the legislators. When the roles are combined, the wielder of those powers tends to see himself as supreme. This leads to an internalization of delegated authority that oversteps the bounds of legitimate government agreements. All power to govern must ultimately be seen as vested in the people who are governed.

The executive, though secondary in power to the legislators, is not limited narrowly to the execution of established laws. Legislators cannot anticipate all laws that will be needed to run a well-ordered society. Thus, some issues must be dealt with as a matter of discretion. It is perfectly appropriate for an executive to exercise this discretion, so long as he does not do so in a way that contradicts the will of the legislators or the general good of the people.[30]

The structure of civic power having been established, it is important to set limits on changes to that structure. Anyone who would gain power over a society by conquest or usurpation would do so despotically. To believe that one's own will justifies the assumption of another body politic is to see oneself as an absolute authority. Absolute authority is antithetical to legitimate civil governance, so there can be no legitimate transfer of power in either of these ways.[31]

To summarize, the Lockean social contract is defined by its focus on the importance of law authorized in pursuit of the common good of the people. All legitimate societies are established by majority rule, and all separate executive and legislative power. Power, once delegated in a given form of government, cannot be transferred by those in whom it is vested. The only exception is in the case of hereditary monarchy. In that case the people have consented to that means of transfer at the outset. The contract is a grant of powers. Executives and legislators can exercise only those powers given to them, and all exercises of power must be to the benefit of the people. Finally, power cannot be claimed by another via conquest or usurpation because this would negate the inherent right of the people to be governed only by their own consent.

Rousseau

Rousseau also believes that the express consent of the people is needed to render legitimate the exercise of civic power. Unlike Locke, however, he rejects the ideal of majority rule. Rousseau agrees with Locke and Hobbes that the state of nature is a state of absolute liberty and complete equality. He disagrees with his antecedents, however, on the necessity of entering into civil society. Force cannot legitimate the formation of a society, as Hobbes supposes, because force makes slaves and slavery is a violation of the essential nature of man. Neither can the will of the majority compel entry into civil society. The will of the majority is nothing more than an enslavement of the minority, and, again, slavery is never permissible.[32]

Entrance into civil society, then, is a matter of convention, not necessity. Rousseau supposes that conditions in the state of nature became so filled with obstacles that men saw cooperation as the best means to pursue their collective ends. The problem, then, is not to discover the law of necessity that will set the terms for the rights to be abandoned in order to enter civil society, but to

> find a form of association which defends and protects with all common forces the person and goods of each associate, and by means of which each one, while uniting with all, nevertheless obeys only himself and remain as free as before.[33]

So, for Rousseau, no rights are surrendered upon a legitimate entrance into civil society. Man in a just civil society has the same rights as man in the state of nature. How, then, is civic life to be distinguished? The answer lies in Rousseau's somewhat puzzling notion of the "general will." Man maintains his rights and moral equality, but he surrenders his natural liberty to do as he pleases and allows his liberties to be constrained by the general will. In this way the moral equality of all persons can be enforced. This exchange garners citizens, among other benefits, the right to "proprietary ownership of all he possesses."[34]

The General Will

Rousseau maintains that if a confederacy of individuals surrenders itself entirely to the collective whole, then no liberties have been lost: "In giving himself to the collective whole, then no liberties have been lost. "[I]n giving himself to all, each person gives himself to no one."[35] Those entering into a social contract together accomplish this goal by means of the general will. "Each of us places his person and all his power in common under the supreme direction of the general will; and as one we receive each member as an indivisible part of the whole."[36]

The general will is the volition of the body politic as an organic whole. It is not, however, an aggregate of all of the requisite individual wills. "In fact, each individual can, as a man, have a private will contrary to or different from the general will that he has as a citizen."[37] Essentially, the general will is the combined will of all citizens with private interests removed. Thus there is a distinction between the general will and the will of all.[38]

The key to understanding the nature of the general will lies in the distinction between private and public interests. Private interests address an individual's particular life plan. Such interests incorporate matters of preference and taste. Public interests address only what is good for the entire society. It seeks not the good of the majority (because pursuit of that good enslaves the minority) but rather the good of all. Whereas an individual will is directed toward the good of the individual, the general will is directed toward the good of the body politic as a whole. Thus, it tends toward equality and not partiality.

Because it seeks the good of all based on the will of all, the general will is necessarily limited. It will not seek to dictate life plans for individuals; it will only proscribe life plans that are not in the best interest of society. The liberty of individual citizens will be curtailed only as necessary to maintain the health of the entire body politic. However, having completely submitted themselves to the general will, citizens of a body politic are inextricably bound to its authority. "A citizen should render to the state all the services he can as soon as the sovereign demands them. However . . . the sovereign cannot impose on the subjects any fetters that are of no use to the community."[39]

Inalienable and Absolute Sovereignty

In civil society, individuals do completely surrender themselves to the general will as sovereign. The authority of the sovereign is absolute but not oppressive. There is, however, a clear distinction between sovereignty and power. Though the sovereignty in a civil society belongs to the general will of the citizens, that sovereignty is executed by a select individual or group exercising the power that is given to them by the state. Whereas power can be transferred or exercised in a way that alienates it from the will of the people, the general will *is* the will of the people. As such, it cannot be alienated from them.[40] It is a contradiction to suggest that one could be enslaved by or alienated from himself.

Power can be divided, sovereignty cannot. The will exercised by executives, legislators, and judges either is the general will or it is not. The will itself is a unified whole. That is not to say, however, that a people are never in error when deliberating the nature of the general will. Such errors can be ameliorated, however, by keeping societies to a reasonable size and by cultivating a citizenry that has sufficient commonality and maturity.[41]

Rousseau agrees with Locke that the power to legislate must be separate from the power to execute laws. "Otherwise, his laws, ministers of his passions, would often only serve to perpetuate his injustices, and he could never avoid private opinion altering the sanctity of his work."[42] Moreover, in a just society, those who are delegated executive or legislative power must maintain focus on the ultimate sovereignty of the general will. Any exercise of power not in accord with the general will is illegitimate. The health of the body politic depends on this separation of sovereign from power.

So long as that separation is maintained, forms of monarchy, aristocracy, and democracy can all be legitimate societies. All forms, however, have intrinsic flaws. Democracies (though a pure democracy cannot exist) have the most direct access to the nature of the general will, but they are prone to a conflation of private and public goods and thereby to civil war. Kings crave absolute sovereign power, and aristocracies tend to perpetuate a class divide between the governors and the governed.[43]

The solution to the problems inherent in the three simple forms of government is to institute mixed governments such as representative democracies or constitutional monarchies. Which hybrid is best for a given body politic will depend on the citizens to be ruled and their circumstances. The best judge of the relative goodness of a society is the number and condition of the people. If the people prosper and multiply in conditions of abundance, the government is most likely a good one. If the converse is true, the government is almost certainly out of line with the general will.[44]

When to Dissolve Civic Bonds

Once a citizen has submitted himself to a body politic, his obedience cannot be retracted so long as the body lives. Bodies politic, however, tend toward disease and decay. Those who exercise power tend to crave the authority behind it. Government authority tends to expand and not contract. This process, though treatable by procedures known as checks and balances, is inevitable. When power in a society alienates itself from the general will, and when that alienation cannot be remedied, the citizens are obliged to remove themselves. A new body politic may be birthed in the same geographic place, but it holds no allegiance to the former one.[45]

To encapsulate, Rousseau argues that no rights are to be given up upon entry into civil society. Certain liberties are removed from the private domain and vested in the public, but because each citizen has an equal share as sovereign, these liberties are never truly alienated. The social contract entered into by the individuals forming a society entail total surrender to the commonwealth, but this is not slavery because it is impossible to be enslaved to oneself. Some individuals become executives or legislators, but neither is sovereign. Actual sovereignty belongs to the general will, the interests of all citizens combined with all elements of purely private interest removed. So long as the general will is followed by legislator and executive, the commonwealth will be just. Inevitably, the powers in a society drift away from the general will and toward personal interests. When this drift becomes irreparable, the society must be dissolved, and a new one forged. For Rousseau, legitimacy is always inextricably tied to the fundamental welfare of the people as a whole.

Kant

Though scholars have debated the matter, Kant does not seem to share Rousseau's belief that human rationality can come to full fruition in the state of nature. This is because, for Kant, reason is the cause of human freedom, and freedom can only be fully manifest in both of its aspects within civil society. For Kant there is a distinction between inner and outer freedom, and neither can come to full fruition without civil government.

> The laws of freedom, as distinguished from the laws of nature, are moral laws. So far as they refer only to external actions and their lawfulness, they are called juridical; but if they also require that, as laws, they shall themselves be the determining principles of our actions, they are ethical. The agreement of an action with juridical laws is legality; the agreement of an action with ethical laws is its morality.[46]

Inner freedom is the foundation of ethics and outer freedom is the foundation of justice. Civil society is needed to preserve the external freedom that is needed to allow our inner freedom to pursue our moral agency. Since the moral worth of human beings lies in their capacity for willing according to the dictates of reason, the exit from the state of nature is a moral duty as much as a matter of practical necessity.

Recall that Kant shares Hobbes's judgment that in the state of nature, there can be no trust in others, with whom one is in a state of constant warfare. This is because, although all have the inner freedom to distinguish right from wrong, there are no external constraints to ensure that all of those in one's midst will choose right action and not atrocity. Without this assurance, there is no possibility of trust, and the need to protect oneself impedes one's ability to act morally. "After all," Kant writes, "war is only a regrettable expedient for asserting one's rights by force within a state of nature, where no court of justice is available to judge with legal authority."[47] The need that motivates the exit from the state of nature, then, is the need for such external constraints. It is the need for public right.

Because only the instantiation of public right allows people to fully realize their potential as moral agents, those in the state of nature have the right to demand that those around them enter civil society. The right to compel those who refuse to seek peace and to exit the state of nature is an exception to our moral duty to never seek harm to others unless we have been "actively injured" by them. "Thus the state of peace must be formally instituted . . . and unless one neighbor gives a guarantee to the other at his request . . . the latter may treat him as an enemy."[48]

Kant justifies the decency of such otherwise impermissible coercion by appeal to permissive laws of pure reason. Whatever reason demands that we do, it also demands that we take the necessary ends to accomplishment. For example, our obligation to develop our talents, gives us a corresponding obligation to discern what our talents are. Otherwise we cannot take conscious measures to develop them. So when the law of nature (our nature as rational moral agents) requires through pure reason that we and all our company exit the state of nature, it also demands that we force the unwilling to exit with us.[49] This is a necessary means to our end because unless all enter civil society, none are.

So we are able to forcibly compel all in our company to enter civil society, but a civil society of what ilk? Kant asserts that a legitimate civil society will follow the "law of universal right." That is to say, it limits human freedom only to the extent necessary to guarantee maximum freedom for all. This means that people in a just society will have as much liberty as is compatible with the same liberty for everyone. This can be accomplished only with the implementation of a constitution.

Valid constitutions institute public right. "Public right is the sum total of those laws which require to be made universally public in order to produce a state of right," Kant writes. "It is therefore a system of laws for a people."[50] Such lawful constitutions delegate the three powers of the state: legislative, executive, and judicial.[51]

Kant echoes Rousseau in his insistence that legislative power authentically belongs only to the will of the people. The common will of the people must author all laws, because virtuous laws by definition can treat no one unjustly. Although we are capable of doing injustice to others, we cannot sincerely will an injustice to ourselves. Hence, when all in a society combine their wills to create a system of law, that system cannot do injustice to any part of the membership that authored it. "Thus only the unanimous and combined will of everyone whereby each decides the same for all and all decide the same for each . . . can legislate."[52]

Though Kant endorses Rousseau's notion of the general will, his exposition of the terms under which the general will may be reliably determined is far more precise. To be able to legislate according to the universal will of the people, citizens must operate under three conditions: (1) they must have the freedom not to obey laws unless those laws were made with their consent; (2) all must be placed in a context of civil equality in which the law applies equally to all citizens; and (3) there must be a protected status of civil independence which prevents dependence of any citizen on the arbitrary will of another.[53] Under these conditions, citizens can and will legislate for the good of all.

Insofar as he maintains that it is for want of laws that produce conditions of justice that people enter civil society, Kant concurs with Locke and Rousseau that the legislative power is supreme. He also accepts Rousseau's assertion that sovereignty belongs solely to the united people. The united people exercise their sovereignty through legislation. That legislation is implemented by the executive and adjudicated by the magistrate.

The legislative, executive, and judicial roles are distinct and none may usurp the defined powers of the others. The ruler is charged with executing the laws of the land. He appoints magistrates to apply the law and ministers to administer the needs of the state. The magistrates apply the law in the courts, but all binding legal pronouncements integrate a jury because the jury represents the people and it is the people who give legal decrees their authority. Otherwise legal decisions could be unduly influenced by the agents of the state.[54]

The establishment of a just state with the attributes outlined above, however, is only the first step toward the institution of a comprehensive system of justice for Kant. States do not exist in isolation but in relation to other states. Therefore, a comprehensive system of justice accounts not only for the internal function of states, but also for interstate relations and relations between all states within one another's spheres of influence. Thus in addition to an account of the internal right of a state, Kant also provides accounts of international right and cosmopolitan right.

International right, justice between individual states, can exist only if the states are lawful. Lawful states are simply those that have constitutions that implement conditions of internal justice. Only lawful states can interact according to the laws of international right because only the citizens of those states have chosen to fully exit the state of nature and eschew war as a sole means to conflict resolution.

Lawful states may follow the united will of their respective citizenries and choose to enter into free association with one another. This essentially places the requisite states into a relationship with one another as artificial persons. States who enter into a federation must be lawful. That is to say, they must have republican constitutions. This ensures that the artificial persons entering into the federation are acting comparably to moral agents. Just as an individual person is constrained by his knowledge of the moral law, a lawful state is constrained by the united will of its citizenry. This ensures that states will not interrelate as uninhibited individuals in the state of nature. Otherwise, as in the state of nature, there can be no trust.[55]

Just as individual persons negotiate a social contract to bring them into a body politic, individual lawful states may enter into a free federation for their mutual interests. This federation serves to constrain the natural tendency of states toward warfare. The states agree to be bound by a set of rules that give the other states a basis of trust for their international policies.[56] The lawfulness of concerned states and their entry into a free federation are the first two definitive articles for perpetual peace.

As a first principle, the states entering into this federation must do so for the sake of preserving peace among them and with no aim of military conquest. Kant enumerates the specific requirements for such federations in terms of this principal goal by outlining them as the requirements for perpetual peace. Kant divides these into preliminary principles, which make the federation possible, and definitive articles, which sustain the federation and bring it to fulfillment.

There are six preliminary requirements. First, no states may make peace with one another while secretly reserving material for a future war. Otherwise the result would be a temporary suspension of hostilities and not true peace. Second, no autonomous state may be acquired as a result of birthright, barter, or bequest. Third, the states will make intentional progress toward the elimination of all standing armies. So long as there are standing armies within a federation of free states, there remains a constant threat of renewed hostilities. Fourth, states may not amass debt to fund foreign policy. The ability to conduct international affairs on the basis of credit renders war-making too uncomplicated and allows executives to make plans for war without the consent of their citizenry. Fifth, states must respect the autonomy of other states and demonstrate that respect by refraining from forcible interference in their governance. Finally, no state engaged in warfare may employ tactics that would make it impossible for other states to trust them in the future. Such tactics include assassinations, the use of poisons (and presumably the modern correlates of nuclear, chemical, and biological weapons), the incitement of treason, and the breach of established treaties.[57]

Having determined the conditions that are presupposed for international right, it is time to consider the third definitive article for perpetual peace, which describes the foundations for the third stage of public right, cosmopolitan right. Just as international right is founded upon a loose federation of free states for the sake of peace, so cosmopolitan right seeks to establish a kind of global social contract.

Whereas international right is strictly a relationship among states, cosmopolitan right is a relationship among people. All people share the earth equally, and as such they have the right to offer commerce and discourse with one another without being treated as enemies by those from other states. "This right, in so far as it affords the prospect that all nations may unite for the purpose of creating certain universal laws to regulate the intercourse they may have with one another, may be termed cosmopolitan."[58] But for the sake of respecting the autonomy of independent states, cosmopolitan right must be limited to conditions of hospitality.[59] That is the final definitive article for perpetual peace and the final form of public right.

So for Kant, justice is possible in civil society only because justice depends upon equitably applied laws that prevent unreasonable constraints on moral agency because of lack of trust. Lawful states express political right. All lawful states are republican, and all hold the unified will of the citizenry to be sovereign. Legislative, executive, and judicial powers must be separated in both body and purpose, and the legislative power (because it embodies the will of the people) will always remain supreme.

In addition to political right, there is a need for international right. International right is expressed by a free federation of lawful states who act so as to engender trust in their interrelations. Finally, the people of the world are due cosmopolitan right. That is the right to engage in commerce and discourse will all other people in the world without fear of being treated as an enemy. Cosmopolitan right is limited by the autonomy of free states and is limited to matters of hospitality. All public right arises from private right, which arises from human moral agency. Moral agency, in turn, arises from rationality. As with the other contractarians, political legitimacy is grounded in human reason.

Rawls

As was demonstrated by his description of the Original Position, Rawls too sees human reason as the foundation of political legitimacy. When rational, equally invested agents who assume a position of ignorance as to their particular circumstances in society deliberate on first principles for a just society, a general intuition about justice arises. All social primary goods—liberty and opportunity, income and wealth, and the bases of self-respect—are to be distributed equally unless an unequal distribution of any or all of these goods is to the advantage of the least favored. This intuition shapes the essential nature of Rawls's comprehensive theory of justice.

The Priority of the Right over the Good

The deliberators arrive at this intuition by inverting the priority of right and good. All of the previous contractarians derived political right from the goodness of (or, in Hobbes's case, goodness for) human agents. Rawls inverts this priority and derives what is good from what is right. Though what he calls a "thin theory of good" is needed to establish the motives of agents in the Original Position, good in both meaningful senses is derived from principles of right. One sense of good is instrumental good; what is good for a society and what is good for a person given his or her rational life plan. The goods that a society or individual may pursue are limited by standards of right (what Rawls will set forth as the two principles of right). The second sense is moral good, and in this sense, too, Rawls sees good as a derivative of right. "Once the principles of right are on hand, we may appeal to them in explaining the concept of moral worth and the good of the moral virtues."[60] In other words, good actions are good because they seek to preserve principles of right.

Because right is more fundamental than good, no appeal to the greater good of society can ever justify the compromise of fundamental rights for any individual.[61] His view of the primacy of political right leads Rawls to assert that a broad set of political rights are inviolable. A just society is one that fosters moral equality in an atmosphere of natural and social inequalities. Rawls concurs with Kant on the significance of human autonomy, the ability to choose one's own ends. Since it is their autonomy that distinguishes human beings from other animals, that autonomy must be respected in any rules that guide human interaction.[62]

So all people are autonomous because of their capacity for rationality, and because as a species they are capable of rationality, they are all morally equal. These three qualities entail that an adequate theory of justice will elucidate justice as fairness.[63] Rationality, autonomy, and equality are the earmarks of those negotiating from the Original Position. From this position, the deliberators reach agreement on two fundamental principles of justice.

The Two Principles of Justice

The first principle holds that "each person is to have an equal right to the most extensive scheme of equal basic liberties compatible with a similar scheme of liberties for others." The second principle deals with distributive justice and asserts that "social and economic inequalities are to be arranged so that they are both (a) reasonably expected to be to everyone's advantage, and (b) attached to positions and offices open to all."[64]

To elucidate the two primary principles of justice, Rawls employs the principles of efficiency and difference. He stresses that these are not themselves principles of justice, but rather principles by which we may better understand and apply the principles of justice. The principle of efficiency, derived from the Pareto principle in economics, states that the system of justice implemented by a society must have no alternatives that improve the condition of some while worsening the condition of none. In other words, any legitimate theory of justice will pursue the two main principles of justice in a way that maximizes outcomes for all without doing so in a way that enhances overall good by sacrificing the needs of a minority of citizens. Again, efficiency must be constrained by justice. No search for efficiency can make the needs of the many justify abuse of the few.[65]

A second elucidating principle employed by Rawls is the difference principle. The difference principle seeks to preserve the autonomy and moral equality of all people in a society. It requires that there be no inequalities except those required to implement the efficiency principle. In other words, inequalities must benefit the least advantaged in a society. It does not do so by transferring inequality, but by balancing it. The "overadvantaged" are burdened to the extent necessary to balance the inequalities implemented by nature or social construction of identities such as gender and race.[66]

Resolution of Conflicts

Rawls acknowledges that there are situations in which the two principles of justice will conflict, and he provides a tool for managing those conflicts. First, liberty is always the priority, and as such the liberty of some can only be compromised if it is necessary to construct a preferable system of overall liberties. The preference for the least advantaged accomplishes this because it does not seek to shift the group enjoying greater liberty. Instead it seeks a system in which the rights of the most advantaged are curtailed to the extent that they are more compatible with comparable liberties for others. The goal is to strengthen liberty and equality even though the measures involved may in microcosm seem to do the opposite. There are two specific cases which illustrate: "(a) a less extensive liberty must strengthen the total system of liberty shared by all; (b) a less than equal liberty must be acceptable to those with the lesser liberty."[67]

The second principle of priority asserts that the principle of justice is prior to the principles of efficiency and welfare:

> The second principle of justice is lexically prior to the principle of efficiency and to that of maximizing the sum of advantages; and fair opportunity is prior to the difference principle. There are two cases:
> (a) an inequality of opportunity must enhance the opportunities of those with the lesser opportunity;
> (b) an excessive rate of saving must on balance mitigate the burden of those bearing this hardship.[68]

In other words, inequalities are designed to give the principle of liberty a wider application. The privation associated with most real-world inequalities perpetuates a kind of master-slave relation in societies. Those with great wealth are able to at least partially determine the scope of life choices available to those with limited access to wealth and other social goods. Under such conditions, great liberty is enjoyed by the privileged, and this extensive liberty is accomplished by depriving the underclasses of comparable access to freedom and wealth.

Such systems narrow the scope of liberty. It is concentrated, usually in the hands of those who are privileged by an accident of birth. Rawls's system seeks to amend such tendencies and bring greater balance to both liberty and wealth. When balance is approached, a wide scope of liberties can be accessed by a wider span of citizens. This is not the greatest good for the greatest number in the aggregate sense, but rather a limit on liberties such that no one takes more than is compatible with leaving as much and as good for all.

The Duty for Civil Disobedience

When citizens of a society come to realize that the principles of justice are being violated, they are obligated to practice civil disobedience as a remedy. The duty to engage in the practice of civil disobedience is a result of an appeal to the public's sense of justice. The people are justified in employing this means so long as three conditions are met: (1) the justice must be substantial and clear; (2) normal appeals through official political channels must have been exhausted in good faith; and (3) there must not be a critical mass of political minorities with comparable claims. Otherwise, the practice of civil disobedience would do a greater injustice by preventing the normal functions of governance. In other words, civil disobedience should not be used as a primary tool for ensuring that the principles of justice are followed. Instead, it is a tool of last resort when lawful citizenship has proved inefficacious.

The goal, after all, is to develop a comprehensive system of law that creates political right by respecting the autonomy of equality of all persons. Since the best way to advance lawfulness is to behave lawfully, deviating from this practice should be undertaken only when an important change would otherwise remain unaccomplished.

To summarize, Rawls believes that right is elementary. It follows directly from our nature as rational beings, and it grounds all considerations of good. A just society is one that respects the autonomy and equality of all people. The good of the many can never justify violating the rights of the few. The only adequate theory of justice is one that treats justice as fairness. Such theories will create the most far-reaching system of liberties that is compatible with equal liberty for everyone, and goods will be distributed equally. Inequalities are justified only if they are necessary to pick the most advantageous system of overall liberties and then only if no one's primary autonomy and equality are violated. Rawls sees only states that enforce strict liberalism and egalitarianism as legitimate.

This is by far the most comprehensive and liberal construction of the social contract. Rawls argues that if it were followed by all nations, there would be no deprivation and thus no cause for social or military unrest. In short, Rawls's view is intended to perfect Kant's account of political right and thereby to ensure international and cosmopolitan right for all legitimate nations. If Rawls is right, it is both practically and theoretically possible to create a just and sustainable collective of nations.

Conclusion

The central idea behind the social contract is that our nature can lead us directly to a substantial understanding of justice. All of the contractarians whose views have been outlined here have the same underlying intuition that there is something about human rationality that sets terms for human social interaction. Humans are able to negotiate and enforce contracts among themselves, and initial social contracts set the terms for political legitimacy. When that capacity is acknowledged, a question arises: If humans, by their very nature, are able to understand justice and legitimacy, why are violations of political right a commonplace experience in public life? In other words, if we have a fundamental understanding of justice, why is injustice so commonplace? The answer lies in the constant competition between our rational and animalistic natures and plays itself out first in what has come to be called the violence of the status quo. This violence is the subject of the next chapter.

Notes

[1] Hobbes, *Leviathan*, chap. 15, p. 109.
[2] Ibid., chap. 14, p. 91.
[3] Ibid.
[4] Ibid., p. 92.

5 Ibid.
6 Ibid., p. 98.
7 Ibid., p. 93.
8 Ibid., p. 106.
9 Ibid., pp. 92–93.
10 Ibid., chap. 15, p. 101.
11 Ibid., p. 107.
12 Ibid.
13 Ibid., p. 108.
14 Ibid., pp. 108–109.
15 Ibid., chap. 17, p. 121.
16 Ibid., chap. 19.
17 Ibid., chap. 18.
18 Locke, *Second Treatise of Government*, chap. 8, secs. 119–122 (pp. 347–349 in *Cambridge Texts in the History of Political Thought*).
19 Ibid., chap. 7, sec. 89, p. 325.
20 Ibid., sec. 96, p. 332.
21 Ibid., chap. 9, secs. 124–126, pp. 350–351.
22 Ibid., secs. 128–131, pp. 352–353.
23 Ibid., sec. 90, p. 326.
24 Ibid., chap. 10, sec. 132–133, pp. 354–355.
25 Ibid., chap. 11, secs. 135–137, pp. 357–359.
26 Ibid., secs. 138–139, pp. 360–361.
27 Ibid., sec. 14, p. 362.
28 Ibid., chap. 12, secs. 143–147, pp. 364–365.
29 Ibid., chap. 13, sec. 152, pp. 368–369.
30 Ibid., chap. 14, secs. 159–161, pp. 374–376.
31 Ibid., chaps. 16–18.
32 Rousseau, *Social Contract*; bk. I, chaps. 3–4, pp. 143–147.
33 Ibid., chap. 6, p. 148.
34 Ibid., chap. 8, p. 151.
35 Ibid.
36 Ibid.
37 Ibid., chap. 7, p. 150.
38 Ibid., bk. II, chap. 3, p. 155.
39 Ibid., chap. 4, p. 157.
40 Ibid., chap. 1, p. 153.
41 Ibid., chaps. 8–10, pp. 165–170.
42 Ibid., chap. 7, p. 163.
43 Ibid., bk. 3, chaps. 3–6, pp. 178–186.
44 Ibid., chaps. 4–9, pp. 186–191.
45 Ibid., chaps. 10–11, pp. 192–195.
46 Immanuel Kant, *Introduction to the Metaphysics of Morals*. "General Introduction to the Metaphysics of Morals." Section 1: "The Relation of the Faculties of the Human Mind to the Moral Laws" Translated by Mary Gregor. (Whitefish, Kessinger Publishing, LLC, 2004). pp. 11–15.

[47] Kant, "Perpetual Peace", p. 96.
[48] Ibid., p. 98.
[49] Ibid., pp. 118–119.
[50] Kant, *Metaphysics of Morals*, pt. 2, sec. 1, par. 43 (p. 136 in *Cambridge Texts in the History of Political Thought*).
[51] Ibid., par. 45, p. 138.
[52] Ibid., par. 46, p. 139.
[53] Ibid.
[54] Ibid., pars. 47–49, pp. 140–142.
[55] Kant, "Perpetual Peace", sec. 2, pp. 98–105.
[56] Ibid.
[57] Ibid., sec. 1, pp. 93–96.
[58] Kant, *Metaphysics of Morals*, pt. 2, sec. 3, par. 62, p. 172.
[59] Kant, "Perpetual Peace", sec. 2, pp. 105–107.
[60] Rawls, *Theory of Justice*, sec. 60, p. 349.
[61] Ibid., sec. 6, pp. 24–30.
[62] Ibid., sec. 77, pp. 441–449.
[63] Ibid., sec. 18, pp. 93–98.
[64] Ibid., sec. 11, p. 53.
[65] Ibid., sec. 12, pp. 59–65.
[66] Ibid., sec. 13, pp. 65–73.
[67] Ibid., sec. 39, p. 220.
[68] Ibid., sec. 46, p. 266.

Chapter Four

Civil Foundations for Terrorism

Most of the attention garnered by terrorist activities in the modern era has been directed toward international terrorism. As I have argued previously, the focus on international terrorism to the exclusion of domestic terrorism is overly narrow and ignores terrorism in its most primitive forms. Recall the definition of terrorism adopted in the first chapter. By "terrorism," I mean the use of threat and violence of deed and word used to coerce for idiosyncratic, criminal, or political purposes. Terrorism so defined also distinguishes between the direct victims of violence and the intended targets of the desired coercion, manipulation, or propaganda.

Note that I do not employ the distinction between lawful and unlawful states. This distinction, if misapplied, can make matters of justice unacceptably arbitrary. In the last chapter, I outlined numerous approaches to governmental legitimacy. The purpose of these approaches is to distinguish between lawful and unlawful states. For this distinction to be meaningful, it must be used normatively and not descriptively. That is to say, a lawful state cannot simply be a state that other states recognize as lawful. Otherwise, the distinction is one of consensus or, more likely, political expediency. To be illuminating, inclusion or exclusion as a lawful state must be examined in terms of justice and injustice. We often refer to "justice systems," by which we mean the application of legislative directives. History is rife with examples of what Martin Luther King Jr. would call a conflict between the laws of humans and the laws of God. Though it is unnecessary to invoke the divine as a means of grounding the distinction between these two notions of justice, there is a useful methodology in the approach. What is the difference between the way we systematize justice and the way we ought to systematize justice? The answer lies in the unifying principles of human reason; and from reason, moral equality and autonomy.

If, then, we define lawfulness in terms of accord with the principles of moral equality and autonomy, it becomes apparent that no existing states are fully lawful. There are no states that do not endorse, or at least permit, the compromise of these principles in practice. That being said, though, clear differences exist among various nations in this regard. Some nations are observably more just than others.

So rather than try to force an unsupported distinction between fully lawful states and unlawful ones, I will context my remarks with a distinction between decent states and indecent ones. Decent states have a constitution that expresses the terms of that society's social contract and contains within it definitive procedures by which the citizenry may draw attention to and seek redress for unjustified transgressions against autonomy and moral equality. Indecent states either do not have such procedures or do not enable their protected application.

What may come to mind at this point is that, according to most social contract theorists, it is equality and autonomy that bring about the need to enter civil society in the first place; there must be constraints on the exercise of equality and autonomy if people are to live together in harmony. This is certainly true, and it is why I define decency in terms of the prevention of unjustified transgressions against equality and autonomy. What is justified is determined by the people in a given society, but there are limits. In Rawlsian terms, there are social structures that no reasonable person would live under if given options. Transgressions that create such structures must have remedy for a society to be considered decent. The precise parameters may differ from people to people, those limits can be determined if reasonable, unforced deliberation is permitted.

Even states recognized as legitimate states by the global community may use terrorism. States have been known to structure their laws so as to create a slave class. Others have delegated rights on the basis of property acquisition or biological sex. Such actions are often enforced within a society not only by law, but by campaigns that engender great fear of change that has no basis in fact or reason. This variety of coercion exemplifies the essential traits of terrorism as classified by the "academic consensus definition" given in the first chapter. Small subsets of the population are made examples of in such a way that society at large is afraid to effect change. In medieval Europe and early colonial America, society was kept in check by the image of the witch. In America in the mid-20th century, the image of the communist functioned in this way. Both were used to instill fear and enforce oppressive social roles upon the populace at large. The motivation in these cases is political and idiosyncratic, the means of control is fear, and the direct targets of violence are not the desired target of manipulation. These represent an insidious and often ignored form of terrorism that I will call the violence of the status quo.

Given human nature, it is not reasonable to expect that peoples will unite and completely eschew the form of terrorism found in the violence of the status quo. It is, however, reasonable to expect states to move toward decency. The significant difference between decent and indecent states in this regard is that, in decent states, there is sufficient liberty invested in the people to allow them to recognize, call attention to, and resolve injustices. But again, the exercise of such allowances requires an informed perspective. In what follows, I will provide a brief account of terrorism as the violence of the status quo. I will then explain why this form of terrorism lays the groundwork for more recognizable forms of terrorist activity. I will argue that the violence of the status quo provides the civil foundations for terrorism.

Violence Begins at Home

The preceding two chapters have outlined alternative conceptions of governmental legitimacy in terms of social agreements by which a people gives consent to be governed. If the supposition that people can be governed only by their consent is a reliable one—which I think is indeed the case, given the power that people have when they unite—then we must consider the conditions when a people are governed in a manner to which they would not rationally assent. The social conditions that arise under governmental illegitimacy but prior to civil war or revolution I will refer to as the violence of the status quo.

Many political theorists have addressed the phenomena commonly known as constituting the violence of the status quo. Noam Chomsky characterizes such conditions in both domestic and international arenas. In contrasting the violence of the status quo from more recognizable conditions of explicit physical violence he writes, "In part it is more subtle, the violence of the status quo, the muted endless terror that we have imposed on vast areas that are under our control or susceptible to our influence."[1]

The violence of the status quo is both cyclical and constant. It has a variety of modes, but all fall under one of two general categories: active violence and passive violence. While these same categories apply to all kinds of violence, both domestic and international, they are often more difficult to recognize in their domestic context. By domestic, I mean not within homes specifically, but within a society in general. In the domestic realm, active violence tends to reinforce passive forms of violence and the passive tend to be accepted as appropriate (or at least inescapable) realities of sex, ethnicity, sexual orientation, or class. The perpetuation of violence of this kind is insidious and malignant.

Varieties of Violence

Active Violence

When we think of acts of terrorism, we usually have in mind active violence—overt aggressive acts intended to inflict physical or emotional harm. The truckload of explosives detonated in the garage of a federal office building, the boat filled with explosives driven into the side of an aircraft carrier, the suicide bomber exploding his weapon in a marketplace, the kidnapper who beheads a soldier or civilian before a video camera and releases the footage to the media: all of these are examples of active violence. However, not all acts of active violence terrorism are as easily recognized. Some governments commit heinous acts against their own people under the guise of maintaining law and order.

Many states are guilty of unjustly punishing peaceful protest and assembly. Access of the people to protest and assembly as a means of redress is a cornerstone of decency as described in the previous section. To brutally suppress them undermines the essential properties of decent nations. These acts, when not necessitated by an immediate danger presented by protesters, are terroristic in nature. The goal is to suppress a political or idiosyncratic viewpoint that is in conflict with societal status quos. The intended targets of the action are not primarily those that directly receive the violence, but rather the larger subset of the population that supports or defends the targeted viewpoints.

Examples of this kind of violence include the 1970 attack on students protesting the Vietnam War at Kent State University in

Ohio. Some students did throw rocks, break windows, and attempt to burn down an unoccupied ROTC building, but overall the protests were peaceful. On the first day, May 3, National Guardsmen bayoneted two men who had yelled obscenities at them from a car. On May 4, Guardsmen fired upon an assembly of students, presumably because the students threw rocks. The nearest student shot was 60 feet away and the farthest more than 700 feet away. Neither the Guardsmen, the assembly, nor the surrounding community was in grave peril from the thrown rocks. Though there had been acts of arson and mob activities in previous days, the particular assembly upon which the National Guard fired was not engaged in any such activities. The violent response was not necessitated by the actions of the protesters.

Moreover, a tape released on May 1, 2007, by one of the survivors is alleged to provide proof that there was an order to fire given to the Guardsmen.[2] This significantly undermines the claim that there was no organized response, just frightened soldiers. If the intent was not to protect themselves or the citizenry from physical harm, and the shootings were not merely random actions of nervous individuals, there was an underlying motivation and that motivation was most likely political. The message the protesters were sending was a threat to the status quo, and by punishing the expression of that message, it was hoped that similar protests would not be pursued in the future.

It is certainly not the case that President Nixon, or Congress, or leaders in the military sent the National Guard in for the purpose of shooting students. To take such overt action would be political suicide. The power of the violence of the status quo is that an atmosphere of suppression of dissent can be created that is as psychologically powerful as a direct order. When political rhetoric casts dissenters as enemies of the state, those who serve to silence the dissenters can be expected to view themselves as patriots.

That the students protesting against the Vietnam War were being cast as dangerous subversives can be seen in reactions to the Kent State shootings by members of the Nixon administration. In a speech to the American Retail Association, Vice President Spiro Agnew characterized the college student protest movement as a "well-publicized barrage of criticism against the principles of this nation."[3] According to the notes of Nixon chief of staff, H. R. Haldeman, the president expressed hope that "this serves to dampen other demonstrations rather than firing them up."[4] Even though the act of violence in question was not planned and then executed, it was hoped that the effect would be to silence dissent. Such attitudes, especially when they are espoused by government officials and community leaders, serve to facilitate a subtle yet cancerous status quo that undermines decency and foments civil unrest.

Inequitable status quos are enforced in non-Western societies as well. In the spring of 1989, students protested peacefully for several weeks at Tiananmen Square in Peking (Beijing), China. The demonstrators sought democratic reform and refused to leave the square until their demands were met. Late on June 3, military tanks entered the square from multiple directions, cutting off escape routes, and fired on the unarmed protesters. Many of the injured were local residents who were not directly involved in the demonstration. Though estimates of the death toll vary by source, even the People's Republic of China concedes that hundreds of civilians were killed. Thousands more were arrested in the aftermath. Again, this fits the academic consensus definition of terrorism because the motivation was political, and the intended targets were not confined to the direct victims of violence. The goal was to suppress opposition to the current government structure by teaching the people to fear even peaceful protest.

On March 8, 2006, hundreds of men and women were beaten by plainclothes police in Iran for celebrating International Women's Day. Ghodratollah Mahmoudi, the commander of security forces, reported: "This gathering was held without an official permit. The response by the security forces prevented the gathering to take on a political dimension."[5] The attack on the peaceful assembly has a political motivation: to create a fear of dissent from the current political and social ideologies endorsed by the government.

Another, often unrecognized form of active domestic violence is the creation and enforcement of laws that relegate individuals to subperson status. Examples of this form of active violence include polling laws that prohibit subgroups of a population from voting based on sex or ethnicity. These laws enforce an inferior status on rational human beings based on qualities that are irrelevant to the exercise of rationality. The inherent contradiction of denying rights that arise from rationality based on irrelevant properties of rational beings is generally recognized and addressed when disenfranchisement laws are enacted. The result is usually an ill-founded attempt to conflate the ignorance that accompanies a lack of education with irrationality. This is a convenient strategy because those with the power to disenfranchise also have the power, on similar grounds, to deny access to education.

In the modern era, passage of laws directly endorsing oppression has declined, but laws institutionalizing inequity are still commonplace. Most focus on women, and, as the policies come under fire on the international stage as human rights violations, the response is often to transform active violence into passive violence. There are far too many examples of this kind of law to give a fair treatment here, but I will mention a few for reference.

In Iran, it is illegal for a woman to apply for a passport without her husband's permission. Iran's constitution also indicates that women who appear without the Islamic Hijab are subject to public lashing of 74 strokes. In Saudi Arabia, women may not leave the country without permission from their male guardian (husband, father, etc.) and are denied direct participation in their own governance. In response to a group of women protesting their status, Sheik bin Jbeir replied: "Appointing women as parliament members is out of the question. Nobody even thinks about it, because the issues the parliament deals with are public matters under the responsibility of men."[6] Similar conditions persist across much of the Arab world.

Arab nations also relegate homosexuals to the political margins. Homosexuality is illegal in all Arab nations and there are frequent arrests for violations of these laws. In 2001, Egyptian courts convicted 23 gay men to severe prison sentences for contempt of religion.[7] Such intolerance is commonplace an generally accepted by Arab societies as a whole.

Although the West has shunned many forms of legally mandated subjugation of women and sexual minorities, others still endure. In the United States, the Equal Rights Amendment, which was first proposed in 1923, has still not been ratified by the 38 states needed to make it the 28th amendment to the U.S. Constitution. The thrust of the bill, encapsulated in its first section is that "Equality of rights under the law shall not be denied or abridged by the United States or by any State on account of sex."[8] Correlatively, as of 2006, 44 of the 50 states have passed laws outlawing marriage rights for same-sex partners. It is difficult to construe these policies as anything other than an effort to disadvantage groups within a society based on their sex or sexual behavior.

As I have said, the interaction between active and passive violence is cyclical. Active violence in protection of the status quo tends to become an integral part of a society's identity. Societies essentially come to understand themselves in terms of the social hierarchy constructed and reinforced by legal practice and armed intervention. That common identity, in turn, becomes embedded in the identities of individuals. The result is a passively enforced alienation that breeds active violence.

Passive Violence

When ideas and identities that alienate people from their own autonomy and dignity become unspoken truths within a society, those who are alienated become victims of passive violence. This alienation often persists and sometimes intensifies long after the overt laws and policies that engender it have disappeared. Passive violence of the status quo is pervasive and can do disastrous harm to not only the individual victims, but to the integrity of the body politic as a whole.

When a subset of the people loses touch with their own civil authority, they also lose touch with their civic responsibilities. In short, passive violence of the status quo creates groups of people with little to lose and little stake in the well–being of their society. It is people who have undergone this transformation that are most susceptible to overt acts of terrorism because they see any change in the status quo as a likely improvement.

The defining characteristic of passive violence of the status quo is internalization. When a society internalizes and socially enforces an inequitable hierarchy of human value, it exacerbates alienation, which eventually erupts into active violence. The internalization is often common to both the respected and affronted factions.

Women across societies tend to see their identity as tied to the role of servant. The "good wife" and the "good mother" social roles imply the propriety of subservience. When a woman enters the workforce, where permitted politically, she must do so apologetically, particularly if she is a mother. Life as a working mother is something that the lower classes must do and that the upper classes are above. The Christian Parent's Network sympathizes with working mothers: "Our heart goes out to single mothers who often have no choice, and must work! When ever possible, the most important thing a mother can do is to be at home with her children during their formative years."[9]

Initially, this seems to be a reasonable position. Children can be expected to benefit from healthy parental influence. The internalized oppression, however, is in the subtext. The implication is not that children need their parents, but that a woman's identity begins and ends with the fulfillment of her duties to child and home. There isn't even the suggestion that it is appropriate for fathers to stay at home. That would, of course, be unnatural.

And the implications go even deeper. Social mobility is firmly tied to earning potential. If women decide that their place is in the home, they are less likely to pursue higher education and professional distinction. In the absence of these, there is little potential for economic independence, and without economic independence there is little access to social and political capital. Moreover, the absence of economic independence leads women to see themselves as inferior to their husbands and deserving of inequitable or even abusive behavior. The cost of rejecting their role as subservient for women without economic power is often financial ruin.

Similarly, communities of ethnic minorities often embrace and reinforce the social stereotypes that disempower them within a society. One particularly heinous example can be found in the United States and the cultural phenomenon of "acting white." This phenomenon was first explored by anthropologist John Ogbu in 1983. He observed that structured inequalities in American society have two elements. The first inequality is in the social power relationships that give greater access to jobs and education to the group with political majority status. The second is a job ceiling that relegates ethnic minorities to menial or nonmanagerial employment.[10] This is characteristic of the internalization of superiority by the respected factions of society.

Primary examples of internalization of inferiority by oppressed factions, according to Ogbu, contribute to what he deems a school failure problem. As in the case of women not seeking higher education to their economic and political detriment, there are forces of internalized oppression among some racial minorities that serve to bring about the same end. Social conditions that engender a sense of inferiority foster a sense among minorities that their ultimate goal is just to survive because they cannot reasonably expect to succeed in the traditional sense.

Ogbu outlines three characteristic behaviors that exemplify the expression of internalized inferiority. The first is the reverse work ethic, which values success gained by manipulating others into working for you rather than working for yourself, much less for whites. Children with this ethic, according to Ogbu, see earning good marks in school as something for whites to do. A second behavior treats every social interaction as an appropriate venue for manipulation. This serves to advance the opinion, often held by teachers and administrators, that black students are destructive to healthy learning environments. Finally, minority students tend to hold skeptical attitudes toward the efficacy of academic success. They see limited opportunities for blacks in society and thus see no justifying benefit for academic effort.[11]

Ogbu has since modified his hypothesis to account for broader attitudes that accompany black cultural outlooks across economic and class lines. He argues that different cultural norms regarding parenting, work ethic, and the expected payoff for learning contribute to a consistent gap between academic performances across the races. According to this revised thesis, bright minority students will intentionally underachieve to be perceived as more acceptable by their peers.[12] Even though the particular scope of his hypothesis has changed, the upshot is the same. When unjust social inequalities become norms for a society, those norms perpetuate themselves by becoming integrated into the social identities of oppressed groups. Again, this breeds a destructive kind of alienation that inevitably results in the outbreak of active violence.

When a society fosters violence of the status quo, terrorism in one or more of its many forms is unavoidable. Groups suffering from such violence have been isolated from their inherent connection to society as ultimate authors of political authority. Not only are alienated individuals more likely to engage in random acts of violence within a society, they are more likely to sympathize with other groups they perceive to be fighting for freedom from similar oppression. But terrorism begins at home.

The Meaning of Terror by Consent

What I have outlined in this chapter is an account of some kinds of injustices within a society that foment civil unrest. Injustices are damaging to the health and integrity of the society that permits them. When people do not see themselves as recognized, valuable parties to the social contract, this degrades the motivation to preserve their society. I think there is good reason to believe that want of this motivation underlies many of the horrors of modern societies. As writer James Baldwin said in *The Fire Next Time*, "The most dangerous creation of any society is the man who has nothing to lose."

Conditions that foster the "nothing to lose" mentality are those that Rousseau would call conditions of alienation. When the bonds of a society are structured such that certain members of that society are stripped of the powers of self-determination and of the consent to be governed, there exists a state of alienation. People do not have what is naturally theirs in virtue of their rationality: autonomy that is as extensive as is compatible with comparable autonomy for all others in society. Where inequalities of power persist in a manner unjustified to preserve maximum liberty for all, segments of the population will see themselves not as sources of governmental authority and authors of societal power, but as characters being determined by external forces. When such conditions are imposed upon naturally autonomous beings, violence inevitably erupts.

Once the conflagration of internal societal violence begins, it requires little fanning to become an inferno that engulfs a society. It is important for the citizenry of any society to bear in mind that alienating people from their power has great potential for disaster. Unless they wish their society to suffer from the disease of violent internal conflict, those who are party to the social contract must not consent to conditions that allow, much less encourage, the alienation of people from their power as autonomous beings.

Do the peoples of the world knowingly consent to becoming the victims of terror? Of course not. But just as the skydiver who fails to carefully pack his chute (out of haste or some motivation other than the desire for personal harm) consents to conditions that will inevitably cause him injury, so the citizenry of a state who consent to conditions that breed alienation consent to an environment that will inevitably lead to terrorism of one form or another. So long as conditions of inequity and deprivation persist and escalate, so will the resort to violence. As those conditions escalate in an increasingly technologically advanced world, so will the appeal to terrorist rebellion escalate and gain greater potential for destruction of colossal proportions.

At this point I return to my earlier assertion about the distinction between lawful and unlawful states. This difference, as I have said, is only practically applicable as a difference in degree. Like Rousseau, I acknowledge that from the moment of its inception, a body politic begins a slide toward illegitimacy. Thus, even nations with the most just of initial social contracts will over time move toward policies that breed violence as a response to injustice. The goal for a global federation of free states, then, cannot be predicated upon a requirement for full lawfulness in the normative sense. Instead, the goal in practice ought to be to move the nations of the world toward constitutions that enforce decency in current and future regimes.

One approach that has, at least ideologically, sought to implement the move toward decency and federation of decent states is that of the United Nations. The UN charter seeks to foster conditions of humane treatment and justice among its member states and sets guidelines for interaction with states that do not meet its guidelines. The United Nations, however, has often been accused of being a "toothless tiger." Nations that do not wish to be so constrained simply refuse compliance. Their refusal generally goes unchallenged if the state has a sufficiently developed military and industrial complex. The United States has often fallen into this category.

The problem of noncompliance with UN guidelines can be addressed in at least two ways. The first would be to give the tiger some teeth. The nations of the world, as artificial persons, could enter into a kind of "meta-contract" with one another and transfer some of their collective powers to the UN so that it could serve to enforce the contract. This approach, however, is unpalatable for reasons voiced by Kant. When a state delegates authority garnered from its citizenry, it alienates the people's power from their direct supervision. Such alienation would presumably be legitimate only in a Hobbesian social contract, and Hobbesian contracts seem an ill fit with modern visions of human nature and human rights. Thus, a strongly conceived and enforced global social contract is not only untenable in a world filled with standing armies; it is also internally inconsistent, given the underlying assumptions of prevailing social contract theory.

Since the need to recognize and respect all people's moral value is assumed in almost all accounts of social contract theory and since a strong global social contract is unsustainable, there must be an alternative means for dealing with indecent states. Otherwise the human race will remain trapped in the cycle of escalating violence because many in indecent societies will see themselves as having no viable alternative to terrorism as a means of conflict resolution. Human reason demands that action be taken in response to indecent conditions wherever they occur. Failure to do so is complicity in the conditions of unrest and violence that inevitably result from injustice and oppression. Because it is the nature of violence to spread, one cannot reasonably expect to remain unharmed while conditions that facilitate violence persist. Just as reason would lead humans to exit the state of nature for the sake of their own liberty and preservation, so reason demands that humans seek conditions of fairness and legitimacy throughout their sphere of influence.

Without choosing a meta-sovereign, as would be the case in a strong global social contract, the response to indecency outside one's own society can be either diplomatic or military. The military approach utilizes a distinction between lawful and unlawful, or rogue, states as a basis for military action. This approach will be addressed in the next chapter. A multifaceted diplomatic approach will be outlined in the final chapter.

Notes

[1] Noam Chomsky, "Philosophers and Public Philosophy," *Ethics* 79, 1 (October 1968): 1.
[2] Christopher Maag, "Kent State tape said to reveal fire order," *New York Times*, May 2nd, 2007.
[3] Robert Semple, Jr., "Nixon Says Violence Invites Tragedy," *New York Times* May 5, 1970.

4 National Archives/Nixon Presidential Materials Project (NPM); White House Special Files; Staff Member and Office Files; H.R. Haldeman's longhand journals; Vol. V, April 17 – July 22, 1980; May 4, 1970, p. 37.

5 Information from Human Rights Watch. Quote is from "Defending Women–Defending Rights" at (www.defendingwomen-defendingrights.org/iran_police-attack.php).

6 *Al-Hayat* (London), October 25, 1999.

7 Christian Henderson, "Lebanese group tackles biggest taboo", Aljazeera.net, January 2006. at (http://english.aljazeera.net/English/archive/archive?ArchiveId=-17652).

8 109th Congress, 1st Session, H. J. RES. 37, March 15, 2005.

9 (http://www.christian-parents.net/family/F107_Should_Mothers_Work.htm).

10 John U. Ogbu, "Minority Status and Schooling in Plural Societies," *Comparative Education Review* 27, 2 (June 1983): 174.

11 Ibid., p. 180.

12 John Ogbu, *Black American Students in an Affluent Suburb: A Study of Academic Disengagement* (Mahwah, NJ: Lawrence Erlbaum Associates Inc. 2003).

Chapter Five
Rogue States

In the preceding chapter, I described social institutions and policies that compromise the integrity of social contracts. I also argued that such institutions and policies both embody a primitive form of terrorism and provide a fertile breeding ground for more recognizable forms. The more decent nations of the world identify themselves as such. They also recognize nations that do not fit that description. In recent decades, this mode of classification has led to a problematic divide that has hindered global progress toward decency. The classification to which I refer is that of the rogue state.

As the Cold War came to a close in the late 20th century, policy makers in the United States were faced with the challenge of reframing the Soviet Union's place on the global political stage without polar opposition to the "evil empire" that had defined that country's place in U.S. rhetoric for decades. One of the primary tools used to execute that reframing was the rogue state designation. Instead of casting itself as the fortification against the spread of communism, the United States became the guardian of democracy in the face of threats from fanatical outlaw regimes.

Now if a nation is to present itself to the world as a guardian against rogue states, it is vital that there be a concrete understanding of the defining characteristic of rogue states. Early attempts to define a rogue state appealed to reference rather than characteristics. Core nations on the list of rogue states have traditionally been Afghanistan, North Korea, Iraq, Iran, Libya, Cuba, and Sudan. Afghanistan and Iraq were removed from the list after the rogue regimes were deposed by the coalition of U.S. and allied forces in recent years. To be useful as a justification for policy decisions, however, the idea of the rogue state needed to be more fully elaborated. The nature of that elaboration evolved symbiotically with the political climate.

Though the concept of the rogue state developed during the Reagan and George H. W. Bush administrations, it did not become a prominent part of public discourse until Clinton's tenure in the White House. A study reported by Mark Strauss, senior editor for

Foreign Policy, estimates that in 1990, the term was used only 20 times by various media outlets, but during 2000 the term was used almost 5,000 times.[1] The idea that the world is made up of lawful and rogue states had become part of the national consciousness.

Because it is grounded in the concepts of human rights and governmental legitimacy, the term rogue state is inherently derogatory. It creates a stark juxtaposition between good and evil societies and presumes to determine which parties in a given conflict are on the side of right. The normativity of the term can present rhetorical and diplomatic challenges for policy makers. In June 2000, Secretary of State Madeleine Albright indicated that the United States would abandon use of the term and instead make reference to "states of concern" because the rogue state designation had outlived its usefulness. This remained official U.S. policy until the rhetorical arena was radically reshaped by the suicide hijackings of September 11, 2001. With this change of outlook came a reinvigoration of the rogue state concept. The executive branch offered a definition. Rogue states are those states that:

- brutalize their own people and squander their national resources for the personal gain of the rulers;
- display no regard for international law, threaten their neighbors, and callously violate international treaties to which they are party;
- are determined to acquire weapons of mass destruction, along with other advanced military technology, to be used as threats or offensively to achieve the aggressive designs of these regimes;
- sponsor terrorism around the globe; and
- reject basic human values and hate the United States and everything for which it stands.[2]

This definition is, not incidentally, cast in specific relation to the values and ideals of the United States. This apparent ethnocentrism is the source of some of the central criticisms of the term and its associated policies. Some of those criticisms will be elucidated later in the chapter. Before considering condemnations of the rogue state policy, however, it is important to reflect on the legacy of intellectual discourse that inspires the term. It is unreasonable to judge a theoretical construct solely on the basis of its practical employment. And although the term "rogue state" has been used primarily by the United States, the distinction between rogue and legitimate states has a firmly established philosophical foundation.

Philosophical Foundations for the Rogue State Designation

Kant envisions the possibility of a permanently peaceful global society in his essay "Perpetual Peace: A Philosophical Sketch". Kant argues that if all states had republican constitutions committed to fundamental respect for human dignity there would be no need for resort to armed conflict of any sort. Rawls's theory of justice as fairness also implies that a world populated by a certain type of social contract structure, in his view liberal democracies, would have no need to resort to war. Their principles have been viewed as idealistic and even utopian. However, as is clear in the preceding analysis, recent times have seen a renaissance and reinterpretation of this view. Some contemporary policy makers argue that any effort to establish meaningful and lasting peace in the world would necessitate a revamping of the current world order.

Both Kant and John Rawls suggest that world peace is most likely to be attained in a world populated by republics rather than a world where dictatorships of one form or another continue to exist. This belief is predicated on the assumption that only societies that recognize the inherent value and dignity of all persons and their pursuant right to self-governance will follow the rules necessary to ensure true peace and not merely the absence of active hostilities.

Kant's Perpetual Peace

Kant argues that for there to be perpetual peace, a state of peace must be formally instituted. This is because there is a clear distinction between peace and the absence of hostilities. Where a mere absence of hostilities exists, there may still be wars being planned or unjust advantage being sought by means that are not openly hostile. There cannot be peace under such circumstances because causes for war continue to be advanced. A good way to conceptualize what Kant has in mind is through the distinction between traditional war and cold war. In the former there are open hostilities and in the later more covert antagonism and planning for future conflicts. Neither is in any real sense a time of peace.

Such formal agreements to peace, claims Kant, can be made only between lawful states.[3] Kant goes on to explain that while, in relations between legal states, one state may only justly engage in hostilities to rectify an active injury sustained by the actions of another state, the same rules do not apply in the case of "lawless" or what are now known as "rogue" states.

> But man (or an individual people) in a mere state of nature robs me of any such security and injures me by virtue of this very state in which he coexists with me. He may not have injured me actively (*facto*), but he does injure me by the very lawlessness of his state (*statu iniusto*), for he is a permanent threat to me, and I can require him to either enter into a common lawful state along with me or to move away from my vicinity.[4]

If, then, the rules governing just behavior between lawful states are different from those governing behavior between lawful states and their lawless neighbors, how are we to make the relevant distinction? Kant defines a legal state as having one of the following types of constitutions:

> (1) a constitution based on the *civil right* of individuals within a nation (*ius civitas*)
> (2) a constitution based on the *international right* of states in their relationships with one another. (*ius gentium*)
> (3) a constitution based on *cosmopolitan right*, in so far as individuals and states, coexisting in an external relationship of mutual influences, may be regarded as citizens of a universal state of mankind. (*ius cosmopoliticum*) [5]

It seems, then, that Kant's definition of a just, defensive war goes beyond the ordinary understanding of defense against an actual and direct injury. We are also justified in defending ourselves from those with whom we share a mutual sphere of influence if they do not, in one way or another, recognize certain basic rights. Those rights, for Kant, seem to be grounded in the recognition of inherent human value and dignity and the correspondent respect for all persons that are inferred from our knowledge of the moral law. I take this to be the case from his preceding critique of soldiery as a profession.

Kant argues that soldiery as a profession is inherently immoral, because "the hiring of men to kill or be killed seems to mean using them as mere machines and instruments in the hands of someone else (the state), which cannot easily be reconciled with the rights of man in one's own person."[6] If the recognition of right(s) is inherent to a lawful society, and only lawful societies are accorded protection against preemptive war, then any society that does not explicitly recognize such rights in a constitution might justly be the target of a preemptive war. (Preemptive in this sense is a defense against a state with no express prohibition against certain behaviors, even if the lawless state has made no direct attack against the nation that would make war on it.)

Individual rights, then, come directly from the moral law. But from where do individuals derive their rights as citizens of a state? Since states are made up of people, the rights are, as was previously stated, grounded in inherent human dignity and value as rational beings. The specific ground for all rights as a citizen is consent. I am obligated to follow no law, other than those recognizable by reason alone, except by my consent. Such consent must be in accord with that which would be "approved by the general will of the people in an original contract."[7]

If the only lawful states are those that recognize the rights of their citizens, and all citizens have their rights grounded in their consent to be governed in certain ways, then all lawful states will be republican in the classical sense. Republican constitutions are, according to Kant, grounded on three principles: (1) the principle of freedom to act in any way that is not unjust for all members of society, (2) the principle of dependence of everyone on a single common legislation, and (3) the principle of equality for everyone as citizens.[8] The important central ideas are the inherent autonomy of persons and the respect they are correlatively due.

Kant's system seems prima facie to provide a possible justification for preemptive war against lawless states. It seems reasonable, then, to argue that war can justifiably be waged for the sake of peace. Lawful states are justified, as a defense against the destruction of lawlessness, to require lawless states to become lawful—to either adopt republican constitutions—or to be removed from any sphere in which they can influence the well-being of lawful countries. In other words, if force is the only effective means, then republican nations may justly use force to rid the world (since we are now in a global era when the behavior of all states effects the behavior of all others) of non-republican states by conversion or annihilation. Just as our obligation to treat others as ends in themselves applies only to rational beings, so our obligation to refrain from offensive war (offensive at least in the direct sense) applies only to nations with a republican constitution.

To follow this apparent implication of the Kantian position is to justify the forced republicanization of all the countries of the world. If dictators were rational, they would not be dictators, and since not rational, they are an inherent danger to world peace. Rational people desire peace, and it is irrational to will an end without willing the necessary means to that end. Thus, our desire for peace, it seems, obligates us to wage war.

Rawls on Just Wars and Illegitimate States

John Rawls's central principle concerning war is that "constitutional democracies do not go to war with one another. This is not because the citizenry of such societies is particularly just and good, but more simply because they have no cause to go to war with one another."[9] The cases in which democratic societies will go to war are very limited according to Rawls. "The crucial fact of peace among democracies rests on the internal structure of democratic societies, which are not tempted to go to war except in self-defense or in grave cases of intervention in unjust societies to protect human rights. Since constitutional democratic societies are safe from each other, peace reigns among them."[10] Again, the implication seems clear. If the world were entirely populated by constitutional democracies, the world would exist in a state of perpetual peace so long as all nations retained their democratic status.

We do not need ideal democracies to perpetuate democratic peace, according to Rawls. Actual democracies can sustain peace with one another provided that they satisfy the five features of a democratic regime. Such societies will engage in war only with nonliberal "outlaw" states in self-defense, defense of their allies, or intervention in severe cases to protect human rights.[11]

If the means to the end of world peace is global democratization, and if world peace is an end that is worthy of such a Herculean task, then a brief description of what constitutes a democracy for Rawls is in order. Liberal democracies have (1) a fair equality of opportunity, especially in education; (2) a decent distribution of wealth (remember that "decency" is a normative term for Rawls) that allows all members of society to take advantage of their essential freedoms; (3) society as an employer of last resort (This means that the government will provide jobs for the involuntarily unemployed if the economy is not able to do so without intervention. Essentially this is Keynesianism.); (4) adequate health care for all citizens; and (5) public financing of elections and other means to ensure that somewhat neutral public information is pervasive on matters of public policy.[12]

Rawls does not believe that legitimately grounded societies have always sincerely acted as such. There is often a sharp distinction between a societies' ideological foundations and its actual conduct. However, for societies that have the theoretical framework for liberal democracy, the extent to which they can achieve "Kant's hypothesis of a *foedus pacificum* . . . depends on how far the conditions of a family of constitutional regimes attain the ideal of such regimes with their supporting elements." As this ideal is approached, the family of liberal democracies "will engage in war only as allies in self–defense against outlaw states."[13] The question we must now ask is, Would Rawls agree with Kant that the mere presence of outlaw states is a threat to any republic such that war against these states is justified on grounds of self-defense?

Rawls rejects the argument that only liberal democracies can sustain human rights over the long term, and he argues for toleration of decent hierarchical societies. Decent hierarchical societies respect the special class of urgent human rights (freedom from slavery, liberty [but not equal liberty] of conscience, security of ethnic groups from mass murder), but do not respect all the ideals of justice upheld in a democratic regime.[14] As such, we cannot make war against any nation unless it is in self-defense (of us or our allies) or it is necessary against an outlaw state that does not respect even the special class of urgent rights.

What Rawls describes as a decent hierarchical state may well fall under the Kantian conception of a republican society, but as that is not an essential part of this analysis, I will not deal with it here. What is significant here is that by his division between decent and outlaw societies, Rawls may well be justifying war against any outlaw state on the grounds that it perpetrates serious violations of human rights. In his principles of just war, Rawls argues that the aim of a just war is a just and lasting peace and that well-ordered societies (liberal and decent) wage war only against outlaw states "whose expansionist aims threaten the security and free institutions of well-ordered regimes and bring about the war."[15] Again, the central distinction between decency and indecency is the recognition of at least some basic autonomy for and dignity of persons.

It seems reasonable to infer that Rawls would support Kant's claim that there are certain kinds of states that, by their very nature, justify war being waged against them by liberal states. Moreover, such war may be the necessary means to the goal of perpetual peace because outlaw regimes, being rational but not reasonable, cannot be brought into the fold of decent societies by education efforts alone. (There are points at which Rawls argues against this idea and in support of such measures as the United Nations, but it seems that if outlaw regimes are by definition those that do not recognize the truth of essential moral principles, education without significant coercion is unlikely to bring adequate change. It is the Will Rogers conception of diplomatic negotiation: "Diplomacy is the art of saying, 'nice doggy' until you can find a rock.")

Criticisms of the Rogue State Designation

Robert Litwak and Noam Chomsky have criticized the use of the rogue state designation. Both argue that the United States has defined the term in such a way as to justify the maintenance of a substantial military presence after the Cold War.

Litwak's objection to the use of the rogue state designation is that it has no basis in international law. The definition of a rogue state is inherently pragmatic, according to Litwak; the particular characteristics that define a rogue state change as changes occur in what is useful for the foreign policy of the United States and her allies.[16] This pragmatic status, he argues, makes the designation an unstable and inherently problematic tool of foreign policy. According to Litwak, the nations of the world rightly see rogue state status as innately arbitrary and thus as no justification for coercive military or economic actions.[17] Though Litwak undoubtedly has a well-substantiated point about the manner in which the designation has been used in recent years, his conclusion that the term is inherently meaningless is inaccurate. Potential for rhetorical abuse does not imply the absence of objective meaning. As has been demonstrated, the essence of the distinction between lawful and rogue states has a sound philosophical underpinning.

In contrast, Noam Chomsky acknowledges that there is a legal foundation for the designation of a state as outlaw or rogue. He cautions, however, that the legal foundation of the term and the actual employment of the term differ greatly. Understood in its broadest sense, writes Chomsky, a rogue state is one that uses military force to oblige its will internationally in a manner that violates international law. Obliging a nation's will internationally could take a number of forms. The threat (or actual employment) of military force could be used to negotiate favorable trade policies, to elicit support in campaigns against other nations or to encourage the acceptance of cultural norms and values. This is by no means an exhaustive list, nor is it inherently unethical to attempt to create favorable conditions for one's own nation in the international arena. The distinction between rogue and lawful is grounded in the means and not in the desired ends.

In terms of international law, a rogue state is one that violates Articles 41 and 42 of the Charter of the United Nations, which is "recognized as the foundation of international law and world order."[18] Articles 41 and 42 give the UN Security Council the authority to determine which acts constitute a threat to peace and to decide how to deal with those threats. "The only exception is Article 51, which permits the "right of individual or collective self-defense" against "armed attack . . . until the Security Council has taken the measures necessary to maintain international peace and security." Apart from these exceptions, member states "shall refrain in their international relations from the threat or use of force."[19] Outlaw states, as defined by international law, are simply those states that do not operate according to the guidelines mandated by the UN Charter.

Though he affirms that there is a clear theory behind the outlaw, or rogue, state designation, Chomsky maintains that the practical use of the term is starkly different from its theoretical foundations.

> The concept "rogue state" is highly nuanced. Thus Cuba qualifies as a leading "rogue state" because of its alleged involvement in international terrorism, but the U.S. does not fall into the category despite its terrorist attacks against Cuba for close to 40 years. . . . The criteria are fairly clear: a "rogue state" is not simply a criminal state, but one that defies the orders of the powerful—who are, of course, exempt.[20]

Chomsky is not alone in his suggestion that the United States is, in fact, a rogue state. William Blum argues that the United States is the ultimate rogue state. "It can be argued—based on the objective facts of what Washington has inflicted upon the world, as described in this book—that for more than half a century American foreign policy has, in actuality, been clinically mad."[21] Is the United States a rogue state? If so, it is arguable that attacks on her and her interests abroad are justified by the same philosophical argument that justifies the war-as-a-means-to-peace argument outlined above.

Whether the foreign policy of the United States establishes it as a rogue state is an open question. The tenets of the debate are valuable even if they do not lead to an irrefutable answer. The debate is grounded in the acknowledgment of fundamental governmental legitimacy. It is that acknowledgment that has the greatest potential to address the acts and conditions that motivate the dispute in the first place. What is most important to draw from the debate is that policies that ignore the veracity and significance of fundamental human rights are primary contributors to the cycles of violence and deprivation that plague modern societies.

So it is reasonable to conclude that the legitimate or illegitimate actions of states set the stage for the evolution of the nations of the world toward peace or their devolution toward warfare and chaos. Wherever there is a reasonable lack of trust in one's neighbors, there will be obstacles that inhibit peaceful international interaction. In short, the distinction between lawful and rogue actions is both firmly grounded in theory and is of practical import. However, since the rogue state designation is demonstrably problematic in execution, if contingently so, it will likely be more productive to separate discussions of legitimacy and lawfulness from more practical discussions to determine the status of particular actions. Though one must never ignore the intrinsic connection between these concepts, a discussion of justified versus unjustified intervention should prove to be a more useful tool for determinations of appropriate international policies.

Rogue States versus Justified Intervention

If Rawls is right, then significant coercion is needed to reform unlawful regimes. Since such regimes by definition are not reasonable and thus do not recognize essential human rights, it is unlikely that such coercion can be purely nonviolent. Admittedly, not all acts of violence are militaristic. As will be addressed in the next chapter, the most pervasive forms of violence are banal and not easily recognizable as violence in the traditional sense. Nevertheless, whether by overt or covert acts of violence, the reform of unlawful regimes seems to require non-peaceable means.

The most direct way to achieve the reform of a rogue state is to eliminate the instigators of unlawfulness. In other words, the most expedient means to regime reform is regime change. Policies of regime change, however, encroach dangerously upon the internationally recognized right of sovereign states to self-determination. To be in accord not only with international law, but also with internationally recognized standards of morality and decency, one state (or a coalition of states) must have clear and compelling reasons for endeavoring to replace the recognized leadership of an autonomous nation. To make an adequate case for regime change, a nation must transcend the rogue state designation and make a case for justified intervention.

A careful examination of the United Nations Charter provisions addressing standards for armed conflict reveals that those standards reflect and embody the central themes of traditional beliefs about the nature of just warfare. The traditional just-war theory derived from the Judeo-Christian intellectual tradition asserts that preemptive wars are never just. Military action against another nation is just if and only if it (1) is undertaken to redress an actual injury; (2) discriminates carefully between combatants and noncombatants; and (3) uses force that is directly proportional to the actual harm. Thus acts of war intended to prevent harm are by definition unjust.

Just-war theory also stringently confines the limits of response to actual harms. Under these constraints, it would not be just, for example, to undertake a large-scale bombing campaign because another nation shot down one of your jets in international or contested air space. Such action would not be proportional to the initial harm (especially since the attack was not undertaken in your home nation and thus did not endanger civilians or domestic infrastructure) because it can be reasonably expected to result in a far greater loss of life than the one or two individuals in the average military jet. Furthermore, the action would not be sufficiently discriminatory because it would not distinguish combatants from noncombatants.

The acceleration of military technology has further complicated the capability to differentiate between just and unjust military actions. Weapons of mass destruction (WMD) make discrimination practically impossible, and the modern war machine is more directly geared toward eradication than proportionality. In these circumstances, it may be necessary to concede the inherent injustice of modern military action without denying that access to these technologies at times gives practical justification to actions that are unjustifiable under the most defensible definitions of justice. In short, modern military technology has necessitated a fundamental distinction between justice and justification.

Jan Narveson makes this point in her essay "Regime Change: The Case of Iraq." She proposes that we recognize the necessity of regime change from external forces under certain circumstances without denying the veracity of established concepts of justice and injustice. She writes, "What is problematic about the idea that regime change might justify invasion, at the most general level, is the uncomfortable plausibility of the thesis that all governments are unjust."[22] Narveson's insight is reasonable given the preceding treatment of social contract theory. If Hobbes's views are excluded (and a case for this will be made in chapter seven), then every current nation is guilty of some violations of a legitimate social contract. Narveson's solution to this problematic admission is also sensible: she proposes that we acknowledge scales of injustice.

Not all violations of a social contract are equal in severity. There are some magnitudes of injustice that duly sanction one sovereign nation's forcible removal of the governor(s) of another. Determining when a significant magnitude of injustice has been reached and the scale of armed response that is acceptable becomes a matter of cost-benefit analysis, according to Narveson. In performing this analysis, she recommends that we employ five necessary conditions:

> 1. the new regime that is intended to replace the older one must be a good deal better than it;
> 2. the costs imposed on the invaded state must somehow be acceptable to its people;
> 3. the costs to the invading state must be acceptable to its own people;
> 4. the objective must be worthwhile to the invading state and to a just world;
> 5. there must be a reasonable prospect of success for the new regime. [23]

Narveson's conditions are well supported and reasonable, and they embrace some of the essential assumptions regarding legitimacy and governance by consent that are central to social contract theory. The first condition emphasizes that it is impermissible for any governor (even an interim governor, as in the case of transition governments during times of regime change) to expect those who are to be governed to submit themselves to conditions worse than those in their former circumstances. The second conditioner reasserts the essential attribute of legitimate government as government predicated on the consent of the people. The third condition affirms that no existing government can exceed the power granted to it by its people. The fourth condition recognizes that our spheres of influence make us members of a global society in addition to our national society and that both kinds of society ought to work toward governmental legitimacy. The final condition reminds us that change imposed from the outside has tenuous chances for success compared to change from within because consent to alter a people's form of government predicated on external force undermines the very dignity and autonomy of persons that justified civic actions should be working toward.

Narveson adds more to the debate than a clarification of how it is possible to clarify social contract intuitions into a program for practical action. She also offers a viable solution to the problematic nature of using the rogue state designation as a justification for military policy. To justify military action by the rogue state status of the object of that action is to inappropriately suggest that there are legitimate and illegitimate nations in the world. Such is inappropriate because the world is currently populated with governments that exceed the authority that would be given to them by any just social contract. That is not to say that all of the nations of the world are on equal footing in regard to justice. There are certainly some nations that are closer to the threshold of justice than others. Still the complexity of this scale approach nevertheless requires that we abandon the overly simplistic rogue state policy.

The Importance of the Underlying Distinction

> Man is born free; and he is everywhere in chains. Those who think themselves the masters of others are indeed greater slaves than they. How did this transformation come about? I do not know. How can it be made legitimate? That question I believe I can answer. —Rousseau, *The Social Contract*

Though it is certainly true, as Chomsky and Litwak argue, that the designation of a state as "rogue" can and has been used for purposes of political expediency, it is important to recognize the validity of the philosophical idea that underlies the political distinction between rogue and lawful states. The purpose of applied social contract theory is not to hypothesize about whether there was an actual state of nature. The purpose of social contract theory, as Rousseau so eloquently cast it, is to determine what can make governance legitimate. Even though the rogue state/lawful state distinction does little to justify current foreign policy by the "more lawful" nations of the world, the distinction is a vital one for addressing the conditions that breed injustice and illegitimacy.

The crucial conditions that contribute to terrorism and other social harms are to be found within domestic affairs, not international ones. Social conditions such as poverty, unjustified curtailing of rights, and limited access to education and other social goods are symptoms of an underlying governmental illegitimacy. Given that, the next chapter will seek to elucidate some of the domestic manifestations of violated social contracts that breed unjustified acts of violence.

Notes

[1] Mark Strauss, "A Rogue by Any Other Name: The Adjustable Language of Foreign Policy," *The Chronicle of Higher Education* 47, 16 (Dec. 15, 2000): B11.
[2] National Security Council Statement V (www.whitehouse.gov/nsc/nss5.html)
[3] Immanuel Kant. "Perpetual Peace: A Philosophical Sketch," in *Kant: Political Writings* (*Cambridge Texts in the History of Political Thought*), ed. Hans Reiss (Cambridge: Cambridge University Press, 1970, 1991), p. 98.
[4] Ibid.
[5] Ibid.
[6] Ibid., p. 95.
[7] Ibid., p. 99.
[8] Ibid.
[9] John Rawls, *The Law of Peoples* (Cambridge, Mass.: Harvard University Press, 1999), p. 8.
[10] Ibid.
[11] Ibid., p. 49.
[12] Ibid., p. 50.
[13] Ibid. p. 54.
[14] Ibid., p. 79.
[15] Ibid., p. 94.
[16] Robert Litwak, *Rogue States and U.S. Foreign Policy: Containment after the Cold War* (Baltimore, Md.: Johns Hopkins University Press, 2000), pp. 47–48.
[17] Ibid.
[18] Noam Chomsky, "Rogue States," in *ZMagazine*, at (www.zmag.org/chomsky/articles/z9804-rogue.html), p. 1.
[19] Ibid.
[20] Ibid., p. 14.
[21] William Blum, *Rogue State: A Guide to the World's Only Superpower* (Monroe, Maine: Common Courage Press, 2000), p. 26.
by William Blum
[22] Jan Narveson, "Regime Change: The Case of Iraq," in *A Matter of Principle*, ed. Thomas Cushman (Berkeley: University of California Press, 2005), p. 58.
[23] Ibid., p. 60.

Chapter Six

Illegitimate Responses to Terrorism

> I don't have to worry about justice; my mission is only to destroy and exterminate, nothing more!
> —Hermann Göring, March 3, 1933.

George Santayana cautioned that "those who do not learn from history are doomed to repeat it," and an analysis of historical responses to illegitimate militaristic action by rogue states and terrorists bears out the truth of this intuition. There have been several categories of response to nontraditional threats to national security. This chapter will examine some historical responses to terrorism (and extremism in general) and critique the effectiveness and long-term effects of such measures.

The Exchange of Domestic Liberty for Security

In the aftermath of the terrorist attack on the port of Ostia in A.D. 68 (discussed in the first chapter), the citizens of Rome enacted a number of measures to ensure their safety. Among these was the Lex Gabinia, which designated Pompey the Great as supreme naval commander. He was also given general control over the empire and full control of the Roman treasury in hope that he would use these powers to defeat those that terrorized Rome. Although the pirates were eliminated from the Mediterranean in less than three months, the power delegated to Pompey was never returned to the people. Instead, Pompey used this power to set up puppet regimes in the Middle East that made him wealthy and the region unstable.[1]

Almost nineteen hundred years later, a similar scenario led to similar results in a very different context. On February 27, 1933, Marinus van der Lubbe, a communist arsonist from Holland, burned the Reichstag to protest capitalism. When van der Lubbe was arrested, Hitler told the press: "The German people have been soft too long. Every Communist official must be shot. All Communist deputies must be hanged this very night. All friends of the Communists must be locked up. And that goes for the Social Democrats and the Reichsbanner as well!"[2]   The next day the Emergency Decree was signed mandating

> restrictions on personal liberty, on the right of free expression of opinion, including freedom of the press; [and] on the rights of assembly and association. . . . Violations of the privacy of postal, telegraphic and telephonic communications and warrants for house searches, orders for confiscations as well as restrictions on property, are also permissible beyond the legal limits otherwise prescribed.[3]

On March 23, the Law for Removing the Distress of the People and the Reich was passed, which brought an end to democracy in Germany.[4]

Both Rawls and Kant have stressed the importance of establishing republican constitutions as a precondition for peace. While instituting government by the people is certainly a necessary step toward domestic and international peace, it is not by itself sufficient. Once constitutions are constructed so as to foster just societies, conditions of decency (as previously defined) must be vigilantly maintained. Benjamin Franklin famously responded to a woman inquiring as to the form of government that had been agreed upon in the Constitutional Convention in Philadelphia in the fall of 1787, "A republic, madam, if you can keep it." Because governments tend to seek the expansion of their power once it is delegated, citizens must exercise their powers so as to maintain the parameters of the original contract. Failure of the citizenry to exercise watchfulness can result in a gravitation toward indecency even in societies with exemplary constitutions.

There are many who argue that it is the constriction of liberties that accompanies traditional anti-terrorism measures that invest terrorists with their most destructive powers. According to this line of reasoning, if terrorists can cause a society to have the rights of the people transferred to the government without reasonable consent, then they have accomplished an alteration of the lives of the citizens of that society that no physical attack could ever directly accomplish. There are a number of examples that could be claimed as support for this argument.

Constitutionally speaking, the United States has one of the most republican constitutions in the world. This same nation, however, practiced the internment of Japanese Americans during the Second World War and Muslim Americans after the attacks of September 11, 2001. In November of 2002, Mamoun Alrifai, a native-born American of Palestinian descent, opened the door to federal investigators who indicated that they needed to search the residence. When Mamoun and his father asked to see a warrant, the agent indicated that they didn't have one. Mamoun responded by asking the agents to leave the premises and indicating that he knew his rights. The agent replied, "As of right now, you have no rights."[5] Alrifai's story puts a human face on what came to be know as the post 9/11 dragnet. According to Muzaffar Chishti, an immigration lawyer and a senior analyst at the Migration Policy Institute, a think tank in Washington, out of 1200 people caught in the dragnet between September 2001 and April 2002, none were shown to have any connection to Al Qaeda or terrorism.[6]

The American Civil Liberties Union has also been a vocal critic of a number of anti-terrorism measures developed in recent years. In 2002, there was an initiative by Attorney General John Ashcroft to create a domestic spying program to be executed by ordinary citizens. The Terrorism Information and Prevention System, also known as Operation TIPS, was set to launch in August 2002. Letter carriers, utility workers, deliverymen and the like were to be enlisted to report suspicious behavior observed in the course of their work. The initiative was tabled in July 2002 after coming under scrutiny from members of Congress. The ACLU maintains that such measures are tantamount to devolution of democracy and a direct violation of fundamental constitutional rights.

The Uniting and Strengthening America by Providing Appropriate Tools Required to Intercept and Obstruct Terrorism (USA PATRIOT) Act of 2001 was passed one month after the 9/11 attacks. Some of the provisions in the act are sensible modifications to current policy given technological realities of the Internet age. Section 103 increased funding for the FBI's Technical Support Center. Section 202 gave the government the authority to investigate and practice surveillance relating to computer fraud and abuse offenses. The capacity for destruction as a result of cyberterrorism supports this expansion of the law as well. Similarly, the Section 206 expansion of the Foreign Intelligence Surveillance Act of 1978 (FISA) to include roving rather than landline based surveillance was reasonable given that cellular communication is becoming the norm rather than the exception.[7] Other provisions, however, are far more troubling.

Section 213 amended Section 3103a of title 18, United States Code, to include a provision for delayed notification to the subject of an executed search warrant. Investigating agencies may delay notification that a warrant has been executed and property searched and/or seized if:

> (1) the court finds reasonable cause to believe that providing immediate notification of the execution of the warrant may have an adverse result (as defined in section 2705);
> (2) the warrant prohibits the seizure of any tangible property, any wire or electronic communication (as defined in section 2510), or, except as expressly provided in chapter 121, any stored wire or electronic information, except where the court finds reasonable necessity for the seizure; and
> (3) the warrant provides for the giving of such notice within a reasonable period of its execution, which period may thereafter be extended by the court for good cause shown.[8]

Section 215 substantially expands access to records under FISA. Formerly, FISA business record authority was limited to common carriers, public accommodation facilities, physical storage facilities, or car rental facilities. Section 215 eliminated the categorical limitations and allows FISA business record subpoenas to be issued to "any person." Furthermore, "any tangible thing" can now be covered by a FISA warrant, not just business records. Finally, Section 215 provides immunity for any business complying with a warrant in good faith and waves the restriction of FISA business record authority to "a foreign power or an agent of foreign power."[9] Essentially, FISA may now issue warrants for anything material from any business foreign or domestic and may guarantee prosecutorial immunity for any business that complies.

When the Patriot Act was reauthorized in 2006 (to extend many of the original provisions that were set to "sunset" in December 2005), there was limited contraction of the new governmental authorities. For Section 215 to be used to gain access to sensitive records (such as library and medical records), the reauthorized act requires the approval of the FBI Director, Deputy Director or Official-in-Charge of Intelligence. This section was also amended to require that relevance of the requested data to an investigation of terrorism or foreign intelligence be demonstrated. The reauthorization also mandated extensive reporting on National Security Letters and roving wiretaps, also enacting a sunset period of four years on the latter.[10]

The case can be made (and has been made by a number of organizations) that these provisions constitute a substantial expansion of governmental authority. The right of individuals to a reasonable expectation of privacy and the right of society to have meaningful oversight of law enforcement officials have been significantly curtailed. This is tantamount to a partial restructuring of the social contract of the United States. Whether this restructuring occurred with the consent of the people through their elected representatives is seriously called into question by the admission of members of congress that the bill was not widely or carefully read prior to the vote for approval.

These are cautionary tales to be sure, and it is similar declines of democracy predicated on fear that likely motivated Franklin to remark in 1755, "Those who would give up essential Liberty, to purchase a little temporary Safety, deserve neither Liberty nor Safety." Note, however, that he does not say there are never exchanges of liberty for security. He speaks instead of essential liberties and temporary safety. As an Enlightenment scholar, Franklin was well aware of social contract ideology and realized that the very entrance into civil society is an exchange of liberty for security.

The key distinction here, again, is the distinction between essential liberties and nonessential liberties. Essential liberties are those that cannot reasonably be ceded to the government. I will offer a fuller explication of the nature of essential liberties in the next chapter, but essential liberties are, in short, those that are necessary to maintain the reasonable autonomy and dignity of all human persons. For the purposes of this discussion, it is sufficient to establish that strict controls on these liberties tend to lead toward more injustice than justice.

In contrast, the nonessential liberties that people sacrifice to live together in society are those which, when exercised by individuals, lead to injustice, discord, or chaos. Such liberties include the right to retribution against those who have wronged them and the rights to create and determine the value of their own coinage. The alienation of these kinds of liberties has been an asset rather than an obstacle to maintaining a just and well-ordered society. The alienation of other kinds of liberties has not been as innocuous.

Other freedoms—freedom from imprisonment in the absence of criminal activity, freedom of expression that does not incite violence, freedom of association, and freedom to access those resources required to live a comfortable life—are not reasonably ceded to civil government. Without these, the governed question whether they would be better served by throwing off the shackles of civil society and fending for themselves. Whether ill advised or not, it is this sort of "nothing to lose and everything to gain" ideology that leads to acts of violence against the structures of civil society itself. A government cannot expect, in the long term, to preserve a good society by removing those qualities that make the society good in the first place. In other words, no leader can build a stable domestic policy on forceful coercion.

Military Response

For reasons similar to those outlined above in regard to domestic policy, there are inherent flaws in any strategy that expects to eliminate terrorism with physical force alone. That being said, brute military reprisal has long been seen as the best response by those nations who find themselves victimized by terrorist attack.

On September 13, 2001, two days after the suicide hijacker attacks on the World Trade Center in New York City and the Pentagon Building in Washington, D.C., the United States promised a strong military response. Deputy Defense Secretary Paul Wolfowitz told the press: "One thing that is clear is you don't do it with just a single military strike, no matter how dramatic. . . . We're going to keep after these people and the people who support them until this stops." Though the sentiment ignores what history has taught about the usefulness of violence in curtailing violence, Wolfowitz was vocalizing what many Americans were feeling and saying in the aftermath of the attacks. Reprisal seemed to be what mainstream America wanted and what many in America thought she needed to heal the psychological wounds the attacks had inflicted. In her article in *Capitalism* magazine, Tara Smith put into words the anger and anguish of her fellow citizens.

> As we mourn the thousands whose lives were so brutally extinguished, much of our grief stems from the knowledge that their lives were wrongly taken. These people did not deserve to die; their families do not deserve to suffer. Those who did this, do.
>
> Military action is never undertaken with relish. It is incumbent on our government, however, charged with the defense of Americans' lives and liberties, to undertake decisive reprisals today with righteous resolve. Our cause is just. If we truly honor the victims of these massacres and if we truly cherish our lives and liberties, we must destroy those who have already destroyed so much.[11]

Smith's response is understandable and arguably justified. Al-Qaeda was considered to be responsible for the attacks, and the organization's leader, Osama Bin Laden, was believed to be hiding in Afghanistan under the protection of the Taliban government. Consequently, the United States launched Operation Enduring Freedom on October 7, 2001. In a news briefing that same day, Secretary of Defense Donald Rumsfeld said that the objectives of the offensive were to wipe out terrorist training camps, to capture or kill al-Qaeda operatives, and to support those groups fighting against the Taliban so that the people of Afghanistan could remove the terrorist-backing regime.[12]

In the first year, the United States and its allies succeeded in accomplishing a number of those goals. The Taliban was displaced from power in several key cities, Hamid Karzai was elected president, and millions of dollars in humanitarian aid was provided to the people of Afghanistan. In spite of these successes, however, little substantive progress has been made in the "war on terror." As of November 16, 2006, the International Security Assistance Force still had not disarmed militias in at least five provinces. A spokesman from the UN maintains that local officials and police refused to help. The UN also reports that the Karzai government refused to render aid: "We can't help you," the UN quoted the government. "Do it yourself."[13] In the Hellmand province, in which Taliban ties are particularly strong, opium production has increased 162 percent since Operation Enduring Freedom began, and it increased 59 percent in 2006 alone.[14] Intelligence indicates that Osama Bin

Laden is still alive and is still leading al-Qaeda in its efforts to plan and execute attacks on America and her allies. In short, the military response to the 9/11 attacks has not made America any less susceptible to attacks from terrorists and has not succeeded in eliminating the forces in Afghanistan that sponsor terrorism. Moreover, the soldiers of NATO's International Security Assistance Force are now embroiled in a battle against extremists and insurgents that has no foreseeable end point.

Is the United States, or any other nation for that matter, justified in taking up arms against those who attack them? There is a good case to be made that they are and in traditional wars in which nation opposed nation, the strategy has proved to be generally effective. Making war on terrorism, however, is very different in kind. Though some terrorist groups do receive support from nations, terrorist operations are generally unofficial and multinational. As such, traditional military responses are far more difficult to direct toward their intended target. It is easy to acknowledge, as most nations did in 2001, that a nation is justified in taking up arms against those who attack them. A far more difficult matter to settle is whether military response to terrorist attacks can be either legitimate or effective.

Appeasement

Common wisdom demands that one never negotiate with a terrorist. The strategy of appeasement seeks to resolve conflicts by granting an aggressor a set of concessions, based on negotiation, in the hope of avoiding armed conflict by eliminating the reason for it. Historical attempts to appease agressors in exchange for a cessation of aggression have been pointed failures. The Allies ceded the Sudetenland of Czechoslovakia to Hitler in 1938 even though he had engaged in blatant violations of the Treaty of Versailles for at least three years. The astonishing act of pacification was a diplomatic failure, and the Second World War ensued.

Attempts at appeasement have also been a component of peace negotiations between Israel and Palestine. None of these have resulted in an acknowledgment from Palestinian officials that Israel has a right to exist. Suicide bombings are still commonplace, and anti-Israeli rhetoric has been a rallying force for extremists in the Middle East.

The appeasement strategy has been shown to be ineffective because it seems to reward acts of atrocity (or the threat of acts of atrocity). Humans respond to rewarded behavior by repeating it. As reason dictates on this matter, history has borne out. Aggressors who make progress on their goals through terroristic attacks tend to repeat rather than refrain from those kinds of acts in the future.

Pacifism

Just as force alone cannot be a successful long-term response to acts of terror, neither can pacifism be. Pacifism, generally, is the belief that all use of force is immoral and therefore unjustified. A true pacifist maintains that no act of violence, not even direct defense of oneself or others can ever be justified. To those who see might as making right, pacifism is weakness rather than opposition.

To avoid oversimplifying, I will point out that there are several varieties of pacifism. Absolute pacifism rejects all violence, including war and personal violence. It embodies the biblical ideal of turning the other cheek and loving those who persecute you. In its most extreme form, absolute pacifism prohibits even direct acts of self-defense. This form of pacifism contradicts our basic instincts toward self-preservation. Though absolute passivism can have secondary effectiveness against the injustices that ground terrorism, in its primary form it does little to inspire terrorists to abandon their efforts. For those who see violence as a necessary response to injustice, absolute passivism is generally seen as weakness.

I acknowledge that absolute passivism can have secondary effectiveness against injustice. This happens when a casualty who refused to defend himself or herself is made a martyr for the cause in question. In such cases, the decedent can become a rallying point to inspire others to action. When this happens, however, the efficacy comes not from the absolute passivism, but from the activists (violent or nonviolent) who utilize the persona of the passvist to aid ideological motivation.

Contingent pacifism eschews war and other forms of aggressive violence in virtue of their practice rather than their essential nature. Modern wars and modern weapons cannot discriminate sufficiently to make any military action adequately proportional or discriminating. Though I think there is merit to these observations philosophically, contingent pacifism has one central flaw as a solution to the problem of terrorism—it proposes no positive plan of action. Pacifism is instead a plan of inaction. As such, it cannot be utilized as an active tool against terrorism.

Nonviolent Resistance

One may object that pacifists, particularly Mohandas Gandhi and Martin Luther King Jr., had a great deal of success with their methods. That assertion overlooks two important distinctions. The first distinction that must be addressed is the distinction between pacifism and nonviolence. Neither King nor Gandhi eschewed the use of force. In fact, they relied upon the force of public opinion and united opposition to accomplish their goals. This is not to say that either was unfaithful to their fundamental philosophy. Both described themselves as practicing nonviolent resistance and both were opposed to inaction in the face of oppression.

King and Gandhi extolled the value of bringing enough pressure to bear on a situation to make negotiation seem worthwhile to the opposing side. Gandhi explicitly rejected the connotation of the phrase "passive resistance," predicated on his belief that true resistance is anything but passive. He preferred the term *Satyagraha*, a combination of *satya* (truth-love) and *agraha* (firmness/force). Passive resistance, argues Gandhi, is different in kind from true civil disobedience.

> *Satyagraha* is not physical force. A *satyagraha* does not inflict pain on the adversary; he does not seek his destruction. A *satyagraha* never resorts to firearms. In the use of *satyagraha* there is no ill-will whatever. *Satyagraha* is pure soul-force.[15]

The difference between true passivism and nonviolent resistance is well illustrated by the actions undertaken by King and Gandhi in their parallel campaigns to gain civil equality for their people. In addition to encouraging Indians to resist laws requiring them to carry ID cards and denying them the right to vote in parliament, Gandhi undertook a number of campaigns directed toward exposing the brutality of British policies in India. Indians had been forbidden to make their own salt and were told they had to buy salt from British manufacturers. Gandhi led 75 followers on 24-day, 250-mile march to the sea to make salt. Gandhi and his group reached the sea on April 5, 1930. Gandhi proceeded to gather salt that had dried on the rocks from the sea spray. His act initiated a chain reaction that had villagers across India taking pans to the sea to gather their own salt. Sixty thousand Indians were jailed in a one-month time period. The culminating event of this protest was a raid on the Dharasana Salt Works. Marchers approached 400 armed guards at the factory. The British guards beat the protesters with the butts of their rifles, injuring 300 and killing 3. When the story was made public, the British were exposed and shamed before the rest of the civilized world. It was the beginning of the end of British rule in India.[16]

Similarly, King sought to expose the brutality of racism in the United States to the rest of the world. In his role as spokesman for the Montgomery, Alabama, bus boycott of 1955, he encouraged his supporters to use their economic power to force the city of Montgomery to end racial segregation. King also led sit-ins at segregated lunch counters and was the chairman of the Freedom Ride Coordinating Committee. One result of the expected violence that the Freedom Riders were indeed subjected to was public outrage, and that outrage led to the enforcement of integration laws.[17]

So neither King nor Gandhi believed in pacifism in the sense of passive resistance. Both believed in active resistance, but without appeal to physical harm or force. Could this strategy be used as a primary solution to world terrorism? The answer, unfortunately, must be no. The crucial factor in the success of the campaigns undertaken by King and Gandhi was the outrage of the British and American people when confronted with acts of brutality and injustice. Their success depended on an at least moderately educated population that understood and embraced the ideals of human dignity and governance by consent. Thus, a campaign of nonviolent action against global terrorism would be viable only if conjoined with efforts to edify those living under outlaw regimes as to their own civil and human rights.

A Look toward a Viable Solution

Having argued that traditional responses to violence are flawed in theory or ineffectual in the context of modern terrorism, it is important to offer a positive alternative to complement this negative analysis. The essential problem with military action, appeasement, pacifism, and nonviolent resistance is that all deal with the manifestations of terrorism rather than its source. Terrorists are motivated to perform heinous acts for the purpose of compelling others to accept and support their ideological goals. What could motivate human beings who ought to be innately aware of the value of human life and dignity to behave so inhumanely? Why try to compel by fear rather than reason?

The answer to these questions can be found in two arenas: the banal violence of societies in violation of the social contract, and foreign policy that perpetuates conditions of desperation and fears of ideological annexation. The former, as described in chapter 5, are present in some degree in all societies and can be found in an extreme form in the outlaw states described in this chapter. Foreign policy, particularly in the modern era, has tended to exacerbate rather than alleviate breaches of governmental legitimacy.

Any effectual effort to address terrorism will address its root causes and do so in a way that does not lead to cyclically intensifying conditions of governmental illegitimacy. Otherwise the only result that can be expected is cyclically intensifying incidents of terror. And in a technological advanced era with myriad alternative for weapons that can bring devastation on a massive scale, that is an increasingly frightening chance to take. Any viable solution will also be multilateral and will address not only conditions that compromise human dignity but also the need to help the citizens of the world understand and take responsibility for their own power to decide how they will be governed.

Notes

[1] Robert Harris, "Pirates of the Mediterranean," *New York Times*, September 30, 2006.
[2] "The Reichstag Burns," *The Rise of Adolph Hitler* at The History Place 1996. (http://www.historyplace.com/worldwar2/riseofhitler/burns.htm).
[3] Ibid.
[4] Ibid.
[5] Mary Abowd. "Growing Fears: Arabs Still Reeling from 9/11 Backlash," *The Chicago Reporter*, December 2002.
[6] *Newshour with Jim Lehrer Online Focus.* "Sept. 11 Dragnet." April 3, 2002. (http://www.pbs.org/newshour/bb/terrorism/jan-june02/dragnet_4-3.html).

Illegitimate Responses to Terrorism 111

[7] Library of Congress, THOMAS archive. (http://thomas.loc.gov/cgi-bin/bdquery/z?d107:h.r.03162:).
[8] Ibid.
[9] Ibid.
[10] Ibid.
[11] Tara Smith, "Justice and Self-Defense: On a Military Response to Terrorist Attacks," *Capitalism,* September 25, 2001. Available at (www.capmag.com/article.asp?ID=1113).
[12] Office of International Information Programs, U.S. Department of State. Available at (http://usinfo.state.gov).
[13] Center for Defense Information. Available at (www.cdi.org).
[14] Ibid.
[15] Mohandas K. Gandhi, "On Satyagraha," in *Nonviolence in Theory and Practice,* 2nd. ed., ed. Robert L. Holmes and Barry L. Ghan (Longgrove, Ill.: Waveland Press, 2005), p. 78.
[16] R. Nanda, *Mahatma Gandhi: A Biography, Complete and Unabridged* (New York: Oxford University Press, 1996).
[17] Civilrights.org.

Chapter Seven

A Return to Legitimacy

> Nonviolence is the answer to the crucial political and moral questions of our time; the need for mankind to overcome oppression and violence without resorting to oppression and violence. Mankind must evolve for all human conflict a method which rejects revenge, aggression, and retaliation. The foundation of such a method is love. – Martin Luther King Jr.

The previous three chapters addressed some serious challenges for which any successful social contract theory must account. There are a number of states that are widely recognized as rogue states by the nations of the "free world," some with very good reason. In recent decades, the effects of terrorist activity have become more extensive, and there is a mounting potential for extremist groups to obtain tools of mass destruction. Furthermore, conditions of deprivation and disenfranchisement persist throughout the world.

Such conditions stimulate extremist ideologies that form the basis of modern terrorism. Communications technologies exacerbate extremism by allowing extremists to spread the message of oppression to the more privileged who are at times motivated to act violently on behalf of the oppressed. The orators who champion violent extremism draw attention to very real injustices that are unrelenting in modern society, but the acknowledgment is cloaked in a common and yet false dichotomy which suggests that the only viable means for effecting significant change to unjust political systems is the perpetration of heinous acts of violence.

The key to establishing bedrock principles for any legitimate social contract is to examine the common understanding of what it is to be in a good society. The two most important concepts of this common understanding are justice and liberty.

We know that humans have a rudimentary understanding of both distributive and retributive justice from a very early age. Any parent who has inadvertently given one child more crackers at snack time than another will almost certainly have the unfairness of this action pointed out to them quickly and passionately. What's more, when children are victims of a perceived wrong, they tend to display a desire for negative consequences to be administered to the individual who wronged them. Not only do we develop a simplistic understanding of distributive and retributive justice in our youth, we also intuitively value it.

There is also a great deal of common experience that suggests humans, beginning in childhood and early adolescence, instinctively understand value liberty as autonomy. From the three-year-old child who wants to "do it myself" to the teenager who can't understand why she is not allowed to "live her own life," there is a broad spectrum of human experience which seems to strongly imply that humans are driven to reject paternalism and other compromises of their personal liberty and autonomy.

There is also good reason to infer that humans value not only their own autonomy, but also the autonomy of others. When they are presented with examples of social liberty and social oppression, people of diverse educational levels, socioeconomic classes, and cultures tend to recognize the difference. Charitable organizations like Amnesty International, Oxfam, and CARE serve as vehicles for individuals who want to aide those who suffer deprivation and injustice. Treatises too numerous to name have hailed the moral significance of freedom, and some, like Mill, have made arguments for a profound connection between freedom and happiness.

Though humans do seem to demonstrate drives for justice and liberty, there are numerous other human drives that cannot be bedrocks for a just society. The drives for violent retaliation, greed, and selfishness are undeniably part of human nature. These drives also have great potential to corrupt societal norms and policies into oppressive paradigms. It is because of these seemingly contradictory facets of human nature that social contract theorists have appealed to reason as a mediating force. Reason allows humans to consider the long–term consequences of their actions and to plan accordingly.

Reason teaches that our overall liberty is maximized when we establish institutions and practices that guarantee the same liberty for all. Where unnatural inequalities persist, the political system is in a temporary equilibrium at best. Because humans desire distributive and retributive justice, and their own freedom, they are in a state of perpetual unrest when that justice or freedom is denied. In some circumstances violent retaliation is immediate. In other cases, peaceful retaliation is attempted. This may at first seem oxymoronic, but as Martin Luther King points out in his 1963 *Letter from Birmingham Jail*, "we know through painful experience that freedom is never voluntarily given by the oppressor; it must be demanded by the oppressed."[1] If peaceful resistance fails, violent retaliation can usually be expected. Given these patterns in human social history, it is not in anyone's long term self interest to seek personal gain through the denial of fair treatment or autonomy of others. The goal of rational individuals who want to maximize their own social goods for the long term ought to be the establishment and/or implementation of a decent social contract in which peaceful means for change can be effectively pursued.

Minimal Requirements for Legitimate National and Global Contracts

Any feasible account of social organization for the world of the 21st century must take account of the reality of global interaction. For most of the nations of the world, communication with people from distant lands is commonplace. International interaction is no longer limited to wealthy travelers, business people, and government officials. This change in conditions necessitates a reevaluation of traditional social contract theory. Citizens must uphold certain conditions in their own nations as always. But now, in addition, an emerging global consciousness requires an analogous agreement among all of the people in this global sphere of influence. Before addressing the specific requirements for these two distinct kinds of contracts, I will discuss the minimal requirements for any legitimate social contract agreement.

Based on the prior discussion of justice as fairness and of liberty as autonomy, I propose that these two concepts must be integrated in a substantive way into the presuppositions of any viable and legitimate social contract. Yet, these terms must be far more carefully elucidated if they are to form the foundations for a society. The fact is that recognizing and having an intuitive idea of justice and liberty, however, are far easier tasks than defining those ideas in such a way as to make them a useful conceptual foundation for legitimate social contracts.

As we have seen in the theories of Hobbes, Locke, Rousseau, Kant, and Rawls there are many different ways of interpreting these essential ideas. Each interpretation brings with it a different theoretical framework and thus a different account of governmental legitimacy. How are we to arbitrate the differences and arrive at a useful set of principles for action? The answer is that there is no pragmatic need to draw the lines of definition too precisely. I argue that many types of contracts could be legitimate and that a global collective of legitimate contracts would serve to ameliorate if not eradicate the root causes of terroristic behavior.

Competing Ideologies

To make a blatantly obvious point, the world is an extremely disparate place. Descriptive relativism, the assertion that different cultures have conflicting ideological values, is accurate. It is not reasonable to suggest that a single social contract is suitable, or even desirable, for all of the different peoples of the world. There are bodies politic for which religion is an integral component of any system of government under which they would wish to operate. For others, any governmental endorsement of religion would essentially undermine the ethnic and religious pluralism they wish to foster. There is also disagreement over how balance of power ought to be achieved. Given these realities, a satisfactory account of governmental legitimacy must endorse a span of contractual frameworks.

Numerous philosophers and political theorists have acknowledged the existence of multiple legitimate social contracts. Again, Kant contends that legal states acknowledge the fundamental value and dignity of all persons. Rawls suggests that fully legitimate states are founded on liberal democratic social contracts. Though certain cornerstone assumptions of liberal democracies are essential for legitimacy, the overall democratic government structure is not, I think, indispensable. I believe that Kant's essential principle for legal states is more compatible with the diversity of human culture than is Rawls's.

As I have said, a breadth of experience shows us that from an early age, humans begin to understand and value justice and autonomy. Following the methodology of the social contract theorists, it is sensible to take what we know about human nature and use it as a basis for abstracting an account of the limits of governmental legitimacy. Using Kant's requirement for the recognition of human rights as a guide, I will show that there are several forms of social contract that respect and foster justice as fairness, and liberty as autonomy. However, not all of the theoretical frameworks that have been examined in this work meet the requirements I have set forth.

Why Not Hobbes?

> They seek to establish systems of government based on the regimentation of all human beings by a handful of individual rulers who have seized power by force. Yes, these men and their hypnotized followers call this a new order. It is not new and it is not order. For order among Nations presupposes something enduring—some system of justice under which individuals, over a long period of time, are willing to live. Humanity will never permanently accept a system imposed by conquest and based on slavery. —Franklin Delano Roosevelt

One conception of the social contract is, I argue, untenable because of both its theoretical and practical implications. There are two fundamental flaws with the Hobbesian conception of the social contract. First, the sovereign is not a party to the contract. Second, Hobbes's grounding assumptions about human nature that justify the scope of rights to be ceded to the sovereign are questionable.

When governors are not parties to the social contract agreement with the governed, the only constraint on their exercise of the power that has been ceded to them (ceded rather than **delegated** because the governed have no established process within the system for reclaiming abused powers) is the fear of revolt. Several problems are inherent in this state of affairs. To begin with, by rightly seeing himself as above the law, the governor is placed in a dichotomy in which his autonomy has a higher status than the autonomy of his subjects. Consequently, when his desires and the desires of his people are in conflict, it will only seem reasonable to choose his will over the people's will. In short, the essence of the contract undermines the autonomy of the governed.

Of course, Hobbes would point out that people are ill suited to autonomy. The very motivation for leaving the state of nature according to Hobbes is to avoid the perpetual warfare that ensues when the violent propensities of human beings are not forcibly restrained. The kind of despotic government Hobbes advocated, however, has not demonstrated a great propensity for stability or prosperity in the modern era.

Up until the late medieval period, despotic rule enjoyed a constant, if fractious tenure in most of the "civilized" world. Though the absolute rule of monarchs was constrained by acts such as the *Magna Carta*, dynastic rule was the rule rather than the exception. Was this system stable? That depends on one's definition of the term. There were nearly constant wars over succession and annexation throughout Europe and the Middle East, but if not stable the form of government was nonetheless persistent.

With the rise of the merchant class in Europe and parts of Asia, the hold of despotism on the status quo of civil governance began to wane. The emergence of capitalism as a viable economic system undermined the foundations of feudalism and paved the way for the genesis of the Industrial Revolution in the mid 18th century. Accompanying these economic and technological evolutions was the ascension of Enlightenment thought. With these changes to the economic and intellectual climate came an increasing intolerance for absolutism.

The English Bill of Rights of 1689 considerably curtailed the power of the crown and completed the transformation of England into a constitutional monarchy. The American Revolution and the subsequent ratification of the U.S. Constitution marked a perceptible shift in Western collective political consciousness. Heretofore (and in fact for some time after) democracy had been viewed as the meanest of all forms of government. Nevertheless, the concept of governance by consent finds vivid expression in the rhetoric of the French Revolution. Robespierre and other architects of the revolution sowed the seeds of revolt by appeal to Rousseauean social contract theory. Numerous scholars argue that the Declaration of the Rights of Man and Citizen of 1789 sowed the seeds for the democratization of modern Western society.

Even where despotism survives, in many nations it endures in a substantially altered form. Reigning in the period just prior to the French Revolution, Charles III of Spain implemented far reaching reforms in his nation. He checked the power of the church and forced the Spanish Inquisition into a state of torpor. He also eliminated numerous restrictions on trade and improved transportation and access to markets. Frederick the Great of Prussia came to the throne during this era as well. He reformed the judiciary and created a comprehensive legal code. Though Frederick's contemporary Catherine the Great was unhesitant to retaliate against perceived enemies, she transformed Russia's political landscape by providing her people with greater access to education and health care and by extending protection for women's rights. Catherine's reforms showed a movement away from tyrannical absolutism even in Russia, where the notion of the rule by divine right persisted into the early 20th century.

I do not contend that tyranny and absolutism disappeared as the Bastille fell, but it is in this period that the notions of the right of individuals to freedom from oppression and governance by consent become steadfast elements in the collective consciousness of the West. The essence of this new consciousness is encapsulated on the Great Seal of the United States. It reads, *"annuit coeptis; novus ordo seclorum"* – God has blessed this undertaking; a new order of the ages. The paradigm had shifted and in this new context those who would be despots found themselves in an increasingly precarious position. With few exceptions, dictatorships in the 19th, 20th and 21st centuries have been marked by violent unrest and volatility.

As absolutism declined colonialism declined as well. This left numerous former colonial regions in Central and South America, and later in Africa, in a state of political ambiguity. In 1808, Napoleon placed his brother Joseph on the throne of Spain. This attempt to shore up imperialism in the face of a contravening political climate was met by massive resistance in the Spanish colonies in South and Central America. Simon Bolivar came to prominence during the struggles against Spanish imperialism. He established the second Venezuelan republic in 1813. Bolivar led Peru as acting dictator, liberator, and president for life. His attempts to institute centralist government met with stiff opposition. In 1827 civil war broke out, dramatically undermining Bolivar's attempts at South American unity. In August of 1828, he attempted to quell resistance by declaring himself dictator. Soon after, he was the object of a failed assassination attempt and retired from public life only to die of tuberculosis two years later. Peru, and much of the rest of

South America, was a society of political unrest for most of the 20th century. Political stability was not established until wide spread democratization swept the continent in the late 20th century. Whether it came from absolutists on the right or Communists on the left, the continent could not find constancy in authoritarianism.

The governments of Pol Pot, Juan Peron, Hugo Banzer, Augusto Pinochet, and Mohamed Siad Barre are examples of failed attempts to establish permanent order with a Hobbesian approach to governance. Barre's failure is of particular note because his flight from Somalia in 1991 has left the nation with no official government for the past sixteen years. The cold war between the United States and the Union of Soviet Socialist Republics dominated the global political stage of the latter 20th century. Both nations supported regime changes throughout Latin America, South America, and the Middle East, and their actions arguably laid the foundations for modern terrorism.

The governments and political movements just mentioned have one thing in common, a fidelity to Hobbes's conception of a legitimate social contract. The goal of institution order was pursued through violence and oppression and the results speak for themselves. Hobbes's contention that the people of a state will best be able to prosper under the iron fist of a nearly all powerful sovereign has become unviable (if it was ever truly viable in the first place). The central argument against a Hobbesian social contract in the modern era is that it represses the naturally evolving tendency toward democratization, thereby creating injustices that fostered deprivation and armed conflict. No legitimate social contract would foster such conditions because rational people would not choose to live under them.

The Spectrum of Legitimate Contracts

Having argued that Hobbesian contracts are not legitimate and having established the two fundamental characteristics of legitimate contracts, I will now provide concrete examples of legitimate agreements to be governed. It is important to keep in mind that unlimited autonomy is not the goal of civil society. In fact, it is unlimited autonomy that is believed to necessitate entry into society in the first place. Where there are no limits on autonomy, there is a constant pressure between people exercising their autonomy, and this pressure leads to instability and conflict. As such, unlimited autonomy prohibits the perpetuation of justice.

As Rawls points out, true liberal democracies are legitimate forms of government. Such government structures keep power in the hands of the governed. As previously explained, Rawls argues that society ought to be structured so as to grant as much autonomy and liberty to the citizens as can be provided for all. (This is anti-utilitarian because Rawls's goal is not to maximize overall liberty, but to limit liberty to an extent that no one's freedom depends on the lack of freedom of another.) Goods must also be distributed equally whenever possible, and where unequally to the benefit of the least advantaged. This society is egalitarian in the strongest sense and clearly respects both justice and personal autonomy. It is not, however, the only form of government that meets this threshold.

Constitutional monarchies can also be structured so as to promote autonomy and justice. The United Kingdom is an excellent example. The terms of the constitution delineate the limits of government in such as way as to promote fairness and respect for autonomy. Even though not strictly democratic, such governments are republican. There are established means through which the governed can limit and check the use of the power they have delegated to the government.

It is fairly noncontroversial to identify constitutionally grounded governments like democracies and constitutional monarchies as conducive to legitimate social contracts. It is as evident that dictatorships have proved to be unfavorable foundations for legitimacy. Such forms of government tend to be essentially Hobbesian and are thus subject to the problems previously identified with that account. The more difficult forms of government to establish as favorable or unfavorable for legitimacy are those that incorporate religious ideologies into their fundamental government structures.

Though some religions and some interpretations of major religious texts have proved to be oppressive, there is no necessary relationship between theocracy and illegitimacy. The primary examples of theoretically leaning governments are those in the Muslim world. It is often thought that a people must give up strong ties to religious identity to live in a faithful Islamic society. But again, the connection is not an essential one. As Asma Barlas and Leila Ahmed argue in separate texts, there are coherent readings of the Qur'an that do not imply female inferiority. Though I cannot discuss their arguments in sufficient detail here to do justice to their arguments, the central idea of their texts is that the Qur'an explicitly requires equal treatment and respect for all human persons. Though social practices in Muslim societies have diverged from this ideal, the divergence is ascribable to a misreading of primary texts. In other words, it is perfectly feasible to outline a legitimate social contract for a decent society that nevertheless embodies and expresses the fundamental values of Islam.[2]

Just as there are coherent readings of Islamic religious texts that do not encourage injustice, there are coherent readings of Christian, Jewish, Hindu, and Buddhist primary texts that are compatible with legitimate social contracts. For the major religions there is no necessary connection between religious observance and problematic inequities. Given that, a people need not reject their religious identity to form a just social contract so long as no group or individuals are forced into belief or observance against their will. As Rousseau points out, tyranny of the majority is unjust, and those who cannot form a coherent general will cannot reasonably expect to enter into a just social contract. The result may be smaller states, but better smaller states than oppressive ones.

Analogous Global Social Contracts

Having established a range of legitimate social contracts for individual states, it is time to return to the issues raised by the modern global sphere of influence. Surely if we share a fundamental bond in terms of our shared rationality, then our obligations to respect that bond do not dissipate at national borders. It is important to stress that any global social contract would be very different in kind from a social contract among the governors of an individual state. First and foremost, the people of the world do not collectively delegate rights and duties to world leaders as a collective. So in this crucial respect, a global social contract could not be a social contract in the traditional sense. Moreover, there is no substantial global general will that could be constructed without subjecting at least some people to the tyranny of the majority. That being said, Kant's elucidation of the "cosmopolitan ideal" lays the groundwork for understanding the requirements for an analog of a social contract for a global society.

Cosmopolitanism

Pauline Kleingeld provides an excellent definition of cosmopolitanism: "It is the view that all human beings share certain essential features that unite or should unite them in a global order that transcends national borders and warrants their designations as 'citizens of the world.'"[3] As she illustrates in her explication, there are numerous instantiations of this principle. Recall that Kant argues that cosmopolitanism must be advanced because we have a moral obligation to refrain from treating others as enemies merely because they are from a foreign land. Our moral obligations extend to all people, regardless of the geographic location of their birth or current residence. Kleingeld identifies this as "moral cosmopolitanism," and it is the form on which I will focus this inquiry.

As he explains in the third definitive article for perpetual peace, Kant believes that cosmopolitanism should be limited to matters of hospitality. That is to say, we should not act immorally toward others purely because they are not members of our body politic. However, the requirements of cosmopolitanism cannot have any greater reach because it is imperative that no citizen be obligated to deny the autonomy of their state. Remember, when individuals consent to form and follow a social contract, they are essentially creating an artificial person, a state. And just as no rational individual can legitimately have his autonomy compromised to any greater extent than is necessary to enable living in harmony with others, so no lawful state can have its autonomy limited except to the degree that is necessary for coexisting with other lawful states in a loose federation. The only strict law that binds states under a single global body politic is the moral law.

I believe that Kant is right to point out the tension between state autonomy and cosmopolitanism. I also agree with his analysis suggesting that indecent states are a threat to the safety and liberty of all peoples within their sphere of influence. Moreover, in this global age, we are all in a common sphere of influence. However, I think the balance between state autonomy and cosmopolitan obligation can be struck in a way that is both more comprehensive and less invasive.

When I say that cosmopolitan duties can be more comprehensive without problematically compromising national autonomy, I am referring to the possibility of nongovernmental diplomatic action. Although requiring a government to abide by an enforced and extensive global social contract may problematically compromise national autonomy, government assent and subjugation are not needed in the modern era. Citizens of different nations have greater knowledge of and access to one another than ever before. Just as a people in a society have the inherent authority to decide how they will be governed as a body politic, so the people of the world have the right (and, in fact, the obligation) to seek to better the circumstances of those living under indecent social contracts.

When governments interact with one another, they do so either militarily or diplomatically. Military attempts to resolve injustices are at the minimum practically ineffective and, in all likelihood, internally inconsistent. You cannot force people to accept responsibility for their own freedom. If governments cannot effectively address problems of terrorism militarily, the alternative is diplomacy. There are, however, limitations on the efficacy of required diplomacy. I will explain the difficulties inherent in these two state-centered approaches to resolving injustices that breed terrorism in more detail.

The Contradiction of War for Peace

In chapter five, I explained the Kantian and Rawlsian accounts of the distinction between legitimate and illegitimate states. If Kant and Rawls are correct, may a nation or collective of nations make war for the sake of making true peace possible? Much has been invested in recent decades in the use of armed forces as a means for obtaining peace among the nations of the world. Some claim that Kant provides a solid philosophical foundation for using armed conflict as a means for peace. I maintain that this plan is both ideologically and practically problematic. Armies are as well suited to peacemaking as men are to childbirth. Neither is built for the assigned task.

We find in Rawls and Kant two rather liberal conceptions of just societies. We also find, explicitly or implicitly, a justification for war as a means to perpetual peace. The question that must now be addressed is, Can a decent nation wage war for the sake of peace and in the name of human rights and autonomy without compromising the very things in its own society that it is trying to eliminate from the other? I argue that it cannot because of the nature of modern warfare, the inability of liberal nations to consistently sustain the level of warfare that would be required by the defense of the principles of just war, and the inherent contradiction of forcing a people to embrace its own autonomy.

First, modern warfare does not adequately discriminate between the three groups in an outlaw state: leaders, soldiers, and citizens. Even precision bombs are not that precise, and a society that does not affirm basic human rights is not above using its own citizens as human shields or even massacring them to drum up bad press for the liberal aggressor. The weapons and tactics of modern warriors, particularly in wars against outlaw states, punish those who are victims of an unjust regime more than it does the perpetrators of the injustice. In the end, the "cure" for the human rights violations that citizens suffer in outlaw states is the violation of their ultimate human right: the right to life itself. Certainly in liberal societies, and perhaps in decent ones, there is a basic (if assumed) principle that we may not take the lives of innocents or victims as a means to any end. That is part of the identity of a liberal democracy.

Second, democracies in practice do not, and arguably cannot, consistently apply either their right to defend themselves and their allies or their obligation to protect those suffering urgent civil rights violations. If Kant is right that all outlaw states are by their very existence an assault on the safety of republics, and if liberal democracies are obligated to defend their citizens, it seems that some sort of forceful negotiation would be used against all outlaw states. If we are to justify war on the grounds of protecting the human rights of those in outlaw regimes, consistency would demand that we "liberate" the peoples of all outlaw states. If you cannot negotiate with an unreasonable man, again some measure of long-term forceful change would be required. No nation, or even group of nations, can sustain that level of warfare without significantly compromising the essential liberties of its people. History has demonstrated this truth.

Third, there seems to be an inherent contradiction in forcing a people to embrace their own autonomy. If autonomy is predicated on rationality (and reasonableness as well in Rawlsian terms), it seems unlikely that a people can be forced to develop the level of rationality requisite for the recognition of individual autonomy. Such attempts have failed in the past. If, as has been argued, liberal democracies must shepherd people into their own autonomy, are the liberal democracies respecting the liberty of conscience of those being shepherded? Is it unreasonable to allow that a people could rationally, and perhaps even reasonably, choose a decent hierarchy over a liberal democracy? More fundamentally, can people be forced to be free? Even if they can, can a government that would bring freedom by force be justly considered a liberal democracy? Consistency seems to demand that the answer be no. Liberal democracies recognize equal liberty of conscience for all persons. I argue that that recognition prohibits the forceful implementation of democracy. If a liberal democracy removes an outlaw regime and cannot force a democratic one, has it in practice bettered the lot of any of those it would have be liberated?

Though I recognize the appeal of the view proposing war as a means to peace, I think that the view is internally inconsistent when applied to (or by) democratic societies. For the reasons explained, I do not think that a liberal democracy can remain true to its essential principles and use war as a means of creating a world suitable for perpetual peace. Should the liberal nations of the world, then, disregard their duties as liberal nations and instead adopt a utilitarian foreign policy shell that would better serve to justify and elicit change in the world? We could, but then we would in large part abandon the concept of inalienable right so essential to our identity as a nation and what we claim we want to share with the oppressed peoples of the world. The myriad incidents of immoral behavior reported at the Abu Ghraib and Guantanamo Bay prisons reveal how quickly the value of human rights can decline, even among democratic peoples, in times of war. Though the goal of ending terrorism is both reasonable and praiseworthy, it cannot be attained by erroneously making monsters out of all of those who oppose you. It is irrational to believe that one can remove tyranny from the world by behaving tyrannically. Nietzsche offers a warning about what can happen with such a means/end approach in his book Beyond Good and Evil: "Whoever fights monsters should see to it that in the process he does not become a monster. And when you look into an abyss, the abyss also looks into you."[4]

Realities and Myths of Modern Terrorism

Modern Terrorism and Capacities for Mass Destruction

The nations of the ostensible "free world" cannot simply declare their support for the establishment of global cosmopolitanism and expect the threat of terrorism to disappear. The threats presented by modern terrorism cannot be as easily calculated or as narrowly contained as was possible in earlier eras. The proliferation of biological, chemical, and nuclear weapons technologies in the Cold War and post–Cold War eras have resulted in the potential for terrorist attacks on a heretofore unimaginable scale. As President George W. Bush expressed in a speech at West Point on June 1, 2002:

> The gravest danger to freedom lies at the crossroads of radicalism and technology. When the spread of chemical and biological and nuclear weapons, along with ballistic missile technology— when that occurs, even weak states and small groups could attain a catastrophic power to strike great nations.

The Weapons of Mass Destruction Commission has acknowledged that terrorist groups are seeking WMDs, particularly tactical nuclear weapons. The commission also recognizes that a terrorist cell is far more likely to use a nuclear weapon if obtained than is a state. There is a relatively unambiguous chain of responsibility for state actions that does not generally apply to terrorist organizations. If nothing else, we know where all the nations of the world are at any given moment.[5] The problem of terrorists with WMDs is a very real one, but the solution to the threat is not to attempt to wipe out individual terrorist organizations. Not only does the increasing decentralization of terrorist cells make such efforts generally ineffective, the results are often counterproductive. Forcible armed suppression tends to expand the reach and appeal of the terrorist approach rather than the contrary. In both the short and long terms, a more viable solution is to "dampen the appetite for nuclear weapons and pave the way for realization of the goal of the

[Nonproliferation Treaty]."[6] I contend that such dampening requires repairing fractured social contracts in societies with insufficient provisions for negotiating fundamental political change without recourse to violence.

Poverty and Terrorism

There are societies in the world in which conditions of oppression and desperation are the status quo and, as I have argued and as experience has shown, under those conditions terrorism flourishes. Many scholars and political activists have taken this correlation as evidence that poverty causes terrorism to flourish. States must be permitted to protect themselves. They are in fact required to do so as part of any legitimate social contract. There is, however, an important distinction between self-defense and armed aggression for the purpose of preventing future threats. Strict security measures, intensive investigative efforts, prosecution of those who participate in or plan to enact terrorist attacks are all appropriate and necessary functions of government. The need for effective defense is more critical than ever before, given the capacities for destruction made possible by modern technology.

Effective defense however requires an accurate diagnosis of the problem. Though the correlation between impoverishment in a society and level of terrorist presence is supported by empirical data, the causal connection between being poor and being a terrorist is not. In fact, research suggests that those joining terrorist organizations tend to have greater access to wealth and education than their fellow countrymen that do not enlist. Poverty and terrorism are not unrelated, but they share a common cause rather than being causally related themselves.

Alberto Abadie of the John F. Kennedy School of Government at Harvard University conducted an extensive study of the relationships between poverty and terrorist activity. Abadie argues that evidence does not support the claim that poverty causes terror. In fact, in countries with similar sets of civil liberties, poor countries do not generate more terrorism than rich countries.[7] His results did show, however, that political freedom does have an effect on terrorism, with an "observed increase in terrorism for countries in transition from authoritarian regimes to democracies."[8] In other words, it is insufficient civil liberty and not poverty that foments terrorist activity. But again, a lack of causal relation does not imply that the variables are unconnected.

Poverty can result from natural disasters or a deficiency of natural resources, but in the age of global trade and outsourced labor markets, the cause of poverty is often an unjust social contract. More than one million people died in the Great Potato Famine that struck Ireland in the 1840s. The blight that afflicted the primary food source directly contributed to the starvation of the Irish people. What is often overlooked, however, is that plenty of food was grown in Ireland in 1846, but most of it was exported to England where it fetched higher prices than the average Irishman could pay. They starved not for lack of available food, but for lack of access to social wealth that would allow them to buy it.

Similarly, the 1998 famine in Bahr El Ghazal in Sudan would have been far less severe if warlord Kerubino Kuanyin Bol had not removed large amounts of grain and livestock and if the government had not subsequently blocked civilian access to humanitarian aide. In the modern era, an underlying cause of famine is almost always oppressive or misguided government policy. No rational person would assent to such social contracts if he was unaware of what his position in society would be.

The awareness that tragedies of deprivation and exploitation are the result of unjust social institutions tends to motivate people to action. The intended goal is usually the disestablishment of the offending institutions (either domestic or foreign), and when the methods undertaken are violent and use fear as a means for change, the result is terrorism. Poverty does not cause terrorism, but both phenomena are often caused by illegitimate social contracts.

Responsibility and Limitations on Means for Change

Earlier I indicated that governments can interact with one another only by means of military force or diplomacy. Given a just global social contract agreement that does not infringe upon state autonomy, there is a wide range of diplomatic actions that states can take. A loose federation of free states such as the UN can commit itself to intervene when extreme conditions of injustice arise. Security forces can be sent in to defend victims of ethnic cleansing or a similar atrocity. Note that there is a clear difference in mission between defense and protection and aggressive military tactics.

States can also commit themselves to serve as intermediaries in negotiations between peoples in conflict. Where deprivation and scarcity of necessary goods are results of natural and not political causes, the wealthier nations of the world may provide technologies and resources that will make it possible for a nation to become self-sustaining.

There are, however, limits to the obligations that governments may accept in terms of a binding global social contract. States cannot be required, or even encouraged, to pursue aggressive military action to effect political change in other nations. It is inconsistent to demand autonomy for one's own nation while simultaneously undertaking actions that deny the autonomy of other nations. Moreover, it is ineffective. A people cannot be reasonably expected to embrace liberation by force. Attempts to achieve liberation in such a way inevitably bring about occupation and dependence rather than liberation and autonomy. Armies undertaking aggressive maneuvers bring destruction and chaos, not infrastructure and order.

It is, however, impossible to deny that, more often than not, it is politics and not nature that dictates conditions of misery and injustice. If governments cannot employ diplomacy or military action to enact political change, what can be done? The answer lies in the nature of the global social contract. As Kant indicates, states must be constrained by cosmopolitanism to the extent that they do not require their citizens to treat others badly simply because the others are from another state. But the primary obligations of cosmopolitanism are not between states, but between persons. I have moral duties to all persons regardless of their ethnicity or geographic locale. The dispensation of these moral obligations, by able citizens and groups of citizens, can address the political forces that engender injustice and thereby terrorism.

In addition to traditional citizen-based relief efforts enacted by such groups as Amnesty International, Oxfam, the International Red Cross, and CARE, there are new means for effecting change made possible by modern technology. Most current humanitarian efforts are reactive. They respond to overt acts of injustice. It is possible, however, for groups of citizens to be proactive. Such groups could utilize available technologies and educational access in the free world to address the root causes that inhibit decency in much of the rest of the world. I cannot provide an exhaustive list of alternatives for such groups, but I will outline one that I think could be very effective in encouraging peoples in indecent societies to take responsibility for their innate power as authors of their own governance.

Implements for Change:
The Internet and Democratization

Again, the pervasiveness of communications technology along with the availability of weapons technology has transformed terrorism. Terrorists today can create a culture of fear in vast populations through relatively small-scale assaults. Nevertheless, there is great potential for advancing human freedom using the same communications technologies that have dramatically amplified the reach of terrorist organizations.

Advances in communications technology in the late 20th and early 21st centuries have brought a large percentage of the people of the world into a global sphere of influence. When an actual or suspected act of terrorism, natural disaster, or celebrity gaffe happens, the information is disseminated worldwide in the span of minutes to hours. It is estimated that 6.5 billion people across the globe used the Internet in 2006.[9] Individuals from different nations who, just a couple of decades ago, would have had no contact with one another are now engaged in daily conversation via blogs and chat rooms on the Internet.

A study published in 2005 by the Berkman Center for Internet & Society at Harvard University found a strong correlation between Internet penetration and level of democratization. Specifically they found that increases in the percentage of a population with access to the Internet were accompanied by measurable increases in primary benchmarks of democratic societies.[10] Still more surprising was their finding that Internet penetration has greater effect on level of democratization than rate of literacy.[11]

This means that some of the same dynamics that have made fear of terrorist attacks almost banal in modern society may also be useful for eradicating some of the root motivations of terrorism. The Internet is potentially an invaluable medium for disseminating information about the existence of social contracts and correlative responsibilities that fall on peoples and their leaders. People in a society do not become empowered by having new powers granted to them. The essential lesson of social contract theory is that the power to govern always ultimately lies in the hands of the governed. Thus, the goal is not to intervene so as to liberate people from the outside. Such measures have a very poor track record of long-term efficacy. The goal is to help people in unjust societies understand that they have the power and the responsibility to liberate themselves.

Rawls is correct in contending that oppressive and unjust regimes, being rational but not reasonable, do not recognize the truth of essential moral principles and thus are unlikely to be motivated by education alone to restructure their societies in a more just and equitable manner. My suggestion, however, does not hold the governors of dictatorial regimes to be the appropriate targets of educational campaigns. Governors in such regimes have a vested personal interest in maintaining injustices and inequities because they benefit from them. Moreover, the rulers are able to use the unrest their policies provoke to justify greater totalitarianism as a means to establishing order. It is the people living under those regimes who would benefit from educational outreach. It is far easier to convince those who suffer from injustice of the moral truths manifested in just societies than it is to convince those who benefit. Most important, grounding in the fundamental precepts of social contract theory (exclusive of Hobbesian theory) teaches that the only way in which a just contract can be negotiated is from within. True revolutions, both violent and nonviolent, can arise only when a people withdraws its consent to continue to be governed in a certain manner. One way in which this aspect of a return to legitimacy can be undertaken is through the use of the Internet, which has been shown to be making great inroads into violent and remote parts of the globe.

The use of the Internet to disseminate notions of governmental legitimacy and consent to be governed in a systematic and officially sanctioned manner would of course have to be accompanied by the efforts of the peoples of the free world to be vigilant in the enforcement of their own social contracts and to promote cosmopolitanism in their domestic and foreign policies. Experience shows us that terrorism flourishes alongside conditions of oppression, ignorance, and deprivation. By addressing the ideologies and policies that nurture these conditions, it is possible to work toward destroying the roots of terrorism. Though a very slow and burdensome process, it is a process I think will prove to be more efficacious than continually pruning the seemingly endless branches of violence that grow from those roots.

Conclusion

I have laid out rudimentary concepts of human freedom as justice and of liberty as autonomy, and I have argued that these concepts offer a promising framework for distinguishing legitimate from illegitimate implementations of social contracts. Some will object that these are Western utopian ideals that are not grounded in real-world experience. In the real world, there have always been stark power differentials; there have always been privileged and underprivileged classes, and those in power have always exploited those without it for the sake of their own comfort and prosperity. These are obvious truths.

However, it is fallacious to suggest that these real-world observations constitute a viable counterargument. I mean "fallacious" quite literally; the objection outlined above commits the naturalistic fallacy: it attempts to derive concepts about the way things ought to be (in a normative sense) from the way things are or have been. Of course human history is filled with instances of cruelty, injustice, inequity, and oppression. Oppression and violence seem to be self-perpetuating. The systems of government that have been implemented up to now seem to have fatal flaws. But there is no reason to conclude from any of these "hard facts" that a less flawed system—one that can put an end to the oppression and violence—is untenable. When Santayana cautioned us that we must either learn from history or be doomed to repeat it, he did not mean that we should throw in the towel and become nihilists. Instead, he was reminding us that if we are willing to diligently and objectively take what lessons we can from the past, then we can build a better future for ourselves and our children.

I have argued that terrorism, and the deprivation and desperation that so often accompany it, arise from violations of legitimate social contracts. I have also argued against using military force as a remedy for terrorism. I do not, however, argue that there is a single form of government that is appropriate for all peoples. There are numerous legitimate social contracts, but all share certain fundamental characteristics. All hold that people are governed only by their consent and that consent to be governed is granted only when reasonable autonomy and right to justice for all persons is guaranteed. The responsibility for enforcing this guarantee falls on the governed; it is they who initially delegate rights and powers to their governors, and it is they who must reclaim and redelegate those rights and powers if they are exercised illegitimately. Just social contracts should also provide a mechanism for such redelegation without violence where possible.

Finally, I have advocated the use of global communications technologies including the Internet to enlighten the people of the world regarding the notions of governance by consent and legitimate conditions under which that consent should be given. Will this dissemination serve as a panacea for the plague of terrorism? Certainly it will not. The global political landscape is dense, complicated, and difficult to navigate even for the most empowered and educated of individuals. However, it is certain that lasting peace will never be achieved until the responsibility for setting the terms of governance is embraced by those who must live under those conditions.

Notes

[1] Martin Luther King. "Letter from Birmingham Jail." *Nonviolence in Theory and Practice*, ed. Robert L. Holmes and Barry L. Gan (Long Grove, Illinois: Waveland Press, Inc., 2005) 101-114. p. 104.

[2] See Asma Barlas, *Believing Women in Islam: Unreading Patriarchal Interpretations of the Qur'an* (Austin: University of Texas Press, 2002); and Leila Ahmed, *Women and Gender in Islam* (New Haven, Conn.: Yale University Press, 1992).

[3] Pauline Kleingeld, "Six Varieties of Cosmopolitanism in Late Eighteenth-Century Germany," *Journal of the History of Ideas* 60, 3 (July 1999): 505–524.

[4] Friedrich Nietzsche, *Beyond Good and Evil,* trans. Helen Zimmern (Buffalo, New York: Prometheus Books, 1989), p. 107.

[5] Weapons of Mass Destruction Commission, *Weapons of Terror: Freeing the World of Nuclear, Biological, and Chemical Arms,* June 1, 2006, Available at (www.wmdcommission.org/files/Weapons_of_Terror.pdf). October 2, 2006.

[6] Ibid.

[7] Alberto Abadie. "Poverty, Political Freedom, and the Roots of Terrorism." *American Economic Review*, 96, 2 (May 2006): pp. 50–56. p. 50.

[8] Ibid., p. 56.

[9] "Internet World Stats: Usage and Population Statistics," Available at (www.internetworldstats.com/stats7.htm)

[10] Michael L. Best and Keegan W. Wade, "The Internet and Democracy: Global Catalyst or Democratic Dud?" Research Publication No. 2005 (Berkman Center for Internet and Society Research Publication Series, Harvard University, October 2005), p. 21. Available at (http://cyber.law.harvard.edu/publications).

[11] Ibid.

❧ BIBLIOGRAPHY

Books

Ahmed, Leila. *Women and Gender in Islam*. New Haven, Connecticut: Yale University Press, 1992.

Barlas, Asma. *Believing Women in Islam: Unreading Patriarchal Interpretations of the Qur'an*. (Austin, Texas: University of Texas Press, 2002.

Blum, William. *Rogue State: A Guide to the World's Only Superpower*. Monroe, Maine: Common Courage Press, 2000.

Filmer, Sir Robert. *Patriarcha and Other Writings (Cambridge Texts in the History of Political Thought)*. Edited by Johann P. Sommerville. Cambridge: Cambridge University Press, 2006.

Fraser, Antonia. *Faith and Treason: The Story of the Gunpowder Plot*. (New York, New York: Anchor Press, 1997.

Gandhi, Mohandas. "On Satyagraha," in *Nonviolence in Theory and Practice* (2nd. ed.). Edited by Robert L. Holmes and Barry L. Ghan, 77-84. Longgrove, Illinios: Waveland Press, 2005.

Hobbes, Thomas. *Leviathan*. 3rd ed. Cambridge: Cambridge University Press, 2000.

Kant, Immanuel. *Conjectures on the Beginning of Human History*. An excellent translation is in *Kant: Political Writings (Cambridge Texts in the History of Political Thought)*. Edited by Hans Reiss. Cambridge: Cambridge University Press, 1991.

Kant, Immanuel. *The Critique of Pure Reason*. Translated by Norman Kemp Smith. New York, New York: St. Martin's Press, 1965.

Kant, Immanuel. *Fundamental Principles of a Metaphysic of Morals*. Edited by Irwin Foman and Herbert W. Schneider. New York, New York: Kessinger Publishing Company, 2005.

Kant, Immanuel. *Kant: Political Writings (Cambridge Texts in the History of Political Thought)*. Edited by Hans Reiss, trans. H. B. Nisbet. Cambridge: Cambridge University Press, 1970, 1991.

Laqueur, Walter. *The New Terrorism: Fanaticism and the Arms of Mass Destruction*. New York, New York: Oxford University Press, 1999.

Litwak, Robert. *Rogue States and U.S. Foreign Policy: Containment after the Cold War*. Baltimore, Maryland: Johns Hopkins University Press, 2000.

Locke, John. *An Essay Concerning Humans Understanding*, in *Clarendon Edition of the Works of John Locke*. Edited by Peter Nidditch. Oxford: Oxford University Press, 1975.

Locke, John. *Two Treatise of Government* (*Cambridge Texts in the History of Political Thought*). Cambridge: Cambridge University Press, 1988.

Nanda, B. R.. *Mahatma Gandhi: A Biography, Complete and Unabridged*. New York, New York: Oxford University Press, 1996.

Narveson, Jan. "Regime Change: The Case of Iraq," in *A Matter of Principle*. Edited by Thomas Cushman. Berkeley, California: University of California Press, 2005.

Ogbu, John. *Black American Students in an Affluent Suburb: A Study of Academic Disengagement*. Mahwah, New Jersey: Lawrence Erlbaum Associates Inc. 2003.

Rauch, Leo. *Kant, Foundations of Ethics*. (Millis, Massachusetts: Agora Publications, Inc., 1995.

Rawls, John. *A Theory of Justice*. Cambridge, Massachusetts: Belknap Press, 1999.

Rawls, John. *The Law of Peoples*. Cambridge, Massachusetts: Harvard University Press, 1999.

Robespierre, Maximilien. *Report upon the Principles of Political Morality Which Are to Form the Basis of the Administration of the Interior Concerns of the Republic*. (Philadelphia, printed and sold at no. 112, Market-Street, 1794. OCLC: 17637510).

Rousseau, Jean-Jacques. *The Social Contract*. in *Rousseau: The Basic Political Writings*. Translated by Donald. A. Cress. Indianapolis, Indiana: Hackett Publishing Company, 1987.

Articles

Abadie, Alberto. "Poverty, Political Freedom, and the Roots of Terrorism." *American Economic Review* 96,2 (May 2006): 50-56.

Michael L. Best and Keegan W. Wade. "The Internet and Democracy: Global Catalyst or Democratic Dud?" *Research Publication No. 2005. Berkman Center for Internet and Society Research Publication Series at Harvard University*. October 2005.

http://cyber.law.harvard.edu/home/uploads/503/12-InternetDemocracy.pdf.
Chomsky, Noam. "Rogue States." *ZMagazine*. http://www.zmag.org/chomsky/articles/z9804-rogue.html.
Chomsky, Noam. "Philosophers and Public Philosophy." *Ethics* 79, 1 (October 1968): 1-19.
Harris, Robert. "Pirates of the Mediterranean." *New York Times*, Sept. 30, 2006.
Kleingeld, Pauline. "Six Varieties of Cosmopolitanism in Late Eighteenth-Century Germany." *Journal of the History of Ideas* 60, 3 (July 1999): 505–524.
Maag, Christopher. "Kent State Tape Said to Reveal Fire Order." *New York Times*, May 2, 2007.
Ogbu, John. "Minority Status and Schooling in Plural Societies," *Comparative Education Review* 27, 2 (June 1983): 168-190.
Schossberger, Cynthia. "Raising a Question—Coercion and Tolerance, in Kant's Politics." in *ethic@,- Florianópolis* 5,2 (December 2006): 165-171. http://www.cfh.ufsc.br/ethic@/et52art3.pdf.
Smith, Tara. "Justice and Self-Defense: On a Military Response to Terrorist Attacks." *Capitalism*. September 25, 2001. http://www.capmag.com/article.asp?ID=1113.

Websites

Internet World Statistics. "Internet World Stats: Usage and Population Statistics." http://www.internetworldstats.com/stats7.htm.
U.S. Department of State: Office of International Information Programs. http://usinfo.state.gov.
Terrorism Research www.terrorism-research.-com/history/early.php.
United Nations Office on Drugs and Crime. http://www.unodc.org/unodc/terrorism_definitions.html).
Weapons of Mass Destruction Commission. "Weapons of Terror: Freeing the World of Nuclear, Biological, and Chemical Arms" June 1, 2006, http://www.wmdcommission.org/files/Weapons_of_Terror.pdf.

Index

A
Al–Qaeda 2, 9, 101, 105–106

B
Bin Laden, Osama 105
Bolivar, Simon 118–119

C
Chomsky, Noam 72, 91–93, 97
consent
    governance by 10–12, 25, 42, 44–46, 49–50, 52–53, 54–56, 66–67
    terror by 77, 80–82 100
cosmopolitanism 62, 121–123

D
democratization and internet penetration 130–132

E
Euskadi Ta Askatasuna (ETA) 8, 9–10

F
Filmer, Sir Robert 17, 25–26

G
Gandhi, Mohandas K. 108–109

H
Hobbes, Thomas
    critiques of 22–23, 116–119
    life 19–20
    major works 20
    views on human nature 20–22
    views on the social contract 42–49
    views on the state of nature 22–23

K
Kant, Immanuel
    life 33
    rogue states and 86–89
    views on human nature 33–36
    views on the social contract 57–63
    views on the state of nature 36–37
King Jr., Martin Luther 1, 70, 108, 109, 112, 114
Ku Klux Klan 3
Kurdistan Workers' Party (PKK) 9

L
League of Nations 3
Liberation Tigers of Tamil Eelam (Tamil Tigers) 9
Litwak, Robert 91–92, 97
Locke, John
    life..24–25
    views on human nature 25–27
    views on the social contract 49–53

views on the state of nature 27–30

N

Narveson, Jan 95–97
Nizari Ismalis 6
nonviolent resistance 108–109, 110

P

pacifism (passivism) 107–108, 109, 110

R

Rawls, John
  life 37
  rogue states and 89–91
  original position 37–39
  principles of justice 64–65, 66
  priority of the right over the good 63–64
  veil of ignorance 38
reason 20, 21, 22, 23, 25, 26–27, 30, 33–35, 36, 57–58, 59, 63, 82, 113
Reign of Terror 5
rogue states
  definitions 85, 86–91
  critiques of the distinction 91–97, 123–126
  political history and significance 84–85, 97, 112
Rousseau, Jean Jacques
  life 30–31
  general will 54–55, 59,
  views on human nature 31
  views on the social contract 53–57

views on the state of nature 32

S

Schmid, A.P. 4–5
social contract
  definition 1, 12
  grant of powers versus limitation of powers contracts 12–15
  state of nature and 17–18,
  violations of
state of nature
  literal and metaphorical interpretations 18–19
  critiques of 17–18
states, decent versus indecent 71, 81

T

terrorism
  definitions 1–5, 70
  history of 5–7
  modern 8–9,
  poverty and 97, 127–128
  religion and 9–10, 120–121
  technology and 7, 8, 126–127, 130
  war on 104–106, 123–126

U

United Nations 3, 4, 81, 92, 94, 105, 128
USA PATRIOT Act 101–103

V

violence of the status quo 72–73, 77–80